Influer

Influence

What it *really* means and how to make it work for you

JENNY NABBEN

Harlow, England • London • New York • Boston • San Francisco • Toronto • Sydney • Auckland • Singapore • Hong Kong
Tokyo • Seoul • Taipei • New Delhi • Cape Town • São Paulo • Mexico City • Madrid • Amsterdam • Munich • Paris • Milan

PEARSON EDUCATION LIMITED
Edinburgh Gate
Harlow CM20 2JE
United Kingdom
Tel: +44 (0)1279 623623
Web: www.pearson.com/uk

First published 2014 (print and electronic)

© Pearson Education Limited 2014 (print and electronic)

The right of Jenny Nabben to be identified as author of this work has been asserted by her in
accordance with the Copyright, Designs and Patents Act 1988.

Pearson Education is not responsible for the content of third-party internet sites.

ISBN: 978-1-292-00475-4 (print)
            978-1-292-00523-2 (PDF)
            978-1-292-00522-5 (ePub)
            978-1-292-00802-8 (eText)

British Library Cataloguing-in-Publication Data
A catalogue record for the print edition is available from the British Library

Library of Congress Cataloging-in-Publication Data
A catalog record for the print edition is available from the Library of Congress

10 9 8 7 6 5 4 3 2 1
17 16 15 14 13

Cover design by Nick Redeyoff

Print edition typeset in 10/15pt ITC Giovanni Std by 30
Print edition printed and bound in Great Britain by Clays Ltd, Bungay, Suffolk

NOTE THAT ANY PAGE CROSS-REFERENCES REFER TO THE PRINT EDITION

Contents

About the author

Jenny Nabben is a highly experienced corporate communications consultant who has worked for over 20 years with global companies including HSBC, Coca-Cola Enterprises, Lloyds and Hays.

Jenny has an MBA and is a Master Practitioner in neurolinguistic programming (NLP) with an expanding international practice of training and coaching clients from a wide range of organisations including financial services, telecommunications, fast-moving consumer goods and not-for-profit.

Jenny has a particular interest in language and neuroscience and in helping organisations to connect with their employees better. Jenny founded Nabben Communications in 2010: www.nabbencommunications.com.

Author's acknowledgements

I'd like to thank all those people who have influenced me and in doing so made this book possible. I will be forever grateful to Caroline Goyder who so generously gave me the opportunity to write the book and who was there every step of the way; you are an inspiration and a true friend. Also to Dr Tamara Russell, my friend and mindfulness teacher; thanks for sharing your knowledge as a neuroscientist and for your insights to help me shape the book.

To my wonderful family in Australia who are always there no matter what – especially to Lee who is one of the best listeners I know and was there on day one; to Anne, Peter, Rob, Kerri and Elizabeth for your support and love. To Gail Ann Dorsey who's always been my creative inspiration. To Lisa Jennings who knows what she did all those years ago. To my UK family; Louise who has been the staunchest of supporters and to Sian, Yvonne, Liz, Helen C, Helen W, Diane, Megan and Abby for your healing hands.

A huge thank you goes to Eloise at Pearson for being the best commissioning editor a first-time author could ever hope for; without your encouragement, guidance and support I would have given up. Also thanks to Natasha Whelan for seeing this through to the end and to Helen MacFadyen for your expert editorial input.

Finally, I want to end where it all started and thank my mother who is a true artist, a great supporter and simply the biggest influence in my life.

Publisher's acknowledgements

The publishers are grateful to the following for permission to reproduce copyright material:

Figure 1.3 Adapted from Arnsten, A FT (2009), *Nature Reviews – Neuroscience*, 10, 410–22. Adapted by permission from Macmillan Publishers Ltd and Nature Publishing Group © 2009. Figure 1.6 from Barsade, S G (2002) The ripple effect: emotional contagion and its influence on group B behaviour, *Administrative Science Quarterly*, 47, 644, copyright © by SAGE Publications, reprinted by permission of SAGE Publications; Figure on p. 56 courtesy of Dr Tamara Russell; Cartoon on p. 110 by permission of Gary Barker Illustration; 'The Orchestra of Recycled Parts' story on p. 17 © Guardian News and Media Limited 2013.

In some instances we have been unable to trace the owners of copyright material, and we would appreciate any information that would enable us to do so.

How to use this book

This book will help you understand the building blocks of influence; the power of language, how to tell your story with passion and how to tune up your own emotional awareness so you can tune in to others.

You'll find a practical step-by-step path and simple daily exercises that will help you turn up your own dial of influence.

You may like to focus on the ideas that are presented in the book and take more of an intellectual approach with the content and theory of the book. This is one type of learning that allows us to understand theoretical and conceptual ideas of influence. If you use this sort of attention, you will be using the frontal lobe of your brain or the executive centre that helps us make intellectual sense of the world. However, the text offers experiential exercises to try out that will engage you at a more emotional and 'felt' sense of learning. If you choose to do this, you will be using more of your limbic system and developing your insight and emotional intelligence. You can test out for yourself whether you think IQ beats emotional intelligence or whether your preference is more for intellectual understanding. Or you might like to do both and contrast and compare the different ways that your brain processes, understands and assimilates information.

Chapter 1

Influence matters

There is nothing either good or bad, but thinking makes it so.

William Shakespeare, *Hamlet*

Outline

This chapter sets the scene: what influence is and why it's so important; why neuroscience helps us understand how influence works; how to set your goal for what you want to achieve.

1. What is influence?
2. What can neuroscience tell us about influence?
3. What motivates us: fight–flight
4. The science of emotions
5. Influence in action

What is influence?

Being able to positively influence others is one of the most important skills for success in our personal and professional lives. But what do we mean by this word influence?

It's a tricky word – both a noun and a verb – something we 'have' and something we 'do'. Like a lot of words, it packs a big punch because it means so many different things to different people. If you do an internet search you will come up with *Time* magazine's annual list of the top most influential people, which in 2013 includes Jennifer Lawrence (actor), Jay

Z (musician, entrepreneur), Malala Yousazai (social activist), Elon Musk (inventor and entrepreneur) and Hilary Mantel (author). These people influence others through their art, their talent, their intellectual genius or their commitment to a cause – they paint a picture of another world, show us what we are capable of and nourish our creative spirit. But it's not just about the talented, the well-connected or the well-educated. Think of people like Rosa Parks, Camila Batmanghelidjh (The Kids Company) and Paul and Rob Forkan (Gandys flip flops) – these are ordinary people who choose to make a difference in their own unique way. While we might look up to pioneers, visionaries and talented souls, we can each turn up the dial on our own personal influence whether we want to garner support for our cause, inspire others to help us, build our business or be a better leader, coach or friend.

Why is influence important in business?

While influence might take years to build, it can also be lost in a heartbeat. The *Time* magazine list in 2004 included names such as Lance Armstrong and Mel Gibson, in 2009 Tiger Woods and in 2011 Dominique Strauss-Khan – but all of these have now suffered a fall from grace. In the past ten years, many industries and institutions have suffered the same fate as, one by one, they have been found to be wanting: a financial system that has turned the global economic system on its head; UK politicians who now experience the lowest level of trust for years; a section of the press that invaded personal privacy for profit; and corporate giants who spend more on green-washing than on safety and economic fairness. In this world of 'always-on' social media, customers, consumers and voters not only switch allegiance but actively spread the word against those who are found wanting. All of these institutions have suffered huge reputational damage and will take years to recover the trust of consumers and voters. Influence is hard won and quickly lost …

The dial of influence

If building our confidence is about having a better sense of our self in the world, influence is about having a bigger effect on the world. The skills of influence are built on finding the balance between heart and head, between using our intellect and using our emotional intelligence, between knowing when to push through and knowing when to yield to others. While it's not about using positional power to get what you want, it's also not about withdrawing your power and being shy of standing firm when you need to. To influence others we need to stand up and be heard, but we also need to sit still and listen deeply to what others have to say. Influence is the sweet spot right in the middle of all these (see Fig. 1.1).

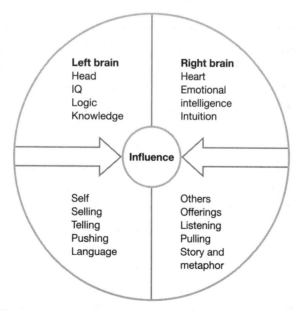

FIGURE 1.1 Influence is the balance between left- and right-brain skills and behaviours.

> **1st rule of influence:**
>
> Find your own sweet spot, focus on those skills that will make the biggest difference in your own life to achieve the things that are most important to you.

What can neuroscience tell us about influence?

Every time you seek to persuade, convince or motivate another person you are looking to affect the way they *think and feel* about your product, your idea or your cause. You want them to say yes, or no, to remain loyal or jump ship, to speak up or speak out. And here's where neuroscience can help – because it provides new insights into how our brain makes meaning of language; why emotions, not logic, drive many of our decisions; why stories trump facts when we want to sell our ideas; and why listening, not talking, can be the most effective influencing skill of all.

Neuroscience is the big kid on the block and punches above its weight as one of the most rapidly expanding fields of scientific research. The growth in this new field of science has been fuelled by the development of new technologies such as functional magnetic resonance imaging (fMRI), electroencephalography (EEG) and chemical neuroimaging (positron emission tomography – PET) to measure changes in brain activity under different conditions. These new technologies allow scientists to map the hidden structures of the brain as well as to study what's really happening across the brain network as groups of neurons fire and communicate. But neuroscience is not so much a discrete study of the grey matter inside our heads, as it is a rich field of knowledge that includes chemistry, computer science, linguistics, mathematics, philosophy, physics and psychology.

While brain science began with the study of a single discrete brain, it has now expanded to include new disciplines such as *interpersonal neurobiology* which studies how two brains in two bodies interact and affect each other at the level of their neurobiology. What this means is that our emotions, language and even our thoughts have the power to affect the brain states of others for better or worse. If we thought that our brain was a single, discrete and private entity, we now suspect it may be more like a single node in a vast complex network. Our brain state not only affects us but also impacts on others via subtle processes that neuroscience is only beginning to explore. This idea is not necessarily new as it is at the heart of ideas suggested by psychodynamic theorists such as Freud and those who followed his approach. What is new is that the neuroscience data is beginning to help us understand the underlying mechanisms of these effects. So what has neuroscience got to do with becoming more influential? And what can it teach us about how we best communicate with others?

In this chapter, we will look at some of the recent findings in the field of neuroscience and their application to language, communication, interpersonal relationships and influencing others. This book will help you build your personal toolkit for influence. Each chapter brings together recent research in the field of neuroscience and builds a picture of what's really happening inside our brains when we communicate and connect with others. The book is intended to provide individuals, business communicators, entrepreneurs and leaders with simple and practical tools to better communicate with and influence others – to offer some hard brain science for why many of the soft skills really are the secrets of true influence.

As a corporate communicator for many years, I became increasingly aware that, although my job involved producing information, much of it was corporate jargon, difficult to understand and unlikely to inspire or motivate employees, customers or the public. Business in general, but large corporate businesses even more so, often embody left-brain thinking; IQ is rated much more highly than emotional intelligence, facts and logic are used more than compelling stories to persuade, leaders are valued for using their heads not their hearts. There is a gap between the style and communication approach of many senior leaders and communicators who wanted to simplify, connect and simply tell the story better. And this is where neuroscience helps by offering communicators and influencers the scientific rationale for why emotions, stories and empathy are more likely to speak to the brains of the audience and therefore inspire, motivate and influence. The table below looks at thinking styles and how they relate to the functions performed by the left and right halves of the brain.

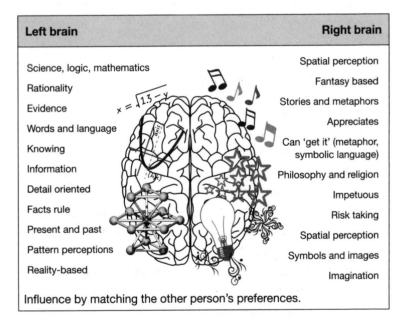

Left brain	Right brain
Science, logic, mathematics	Spatial perception
Rationality	Fantasy based
Evidence	Stories and metaphors
Words and language	Appreciates
Knowing	Can 'get it' (metaphor, symbolic language)
Information	Philosophy and religion
Detail oriented	Impetuous
Facts rule	Risk taking
Present and past	Spatial perception
Pattern perceptions	Symbols and images
Reality-based	Imagination

Influence by matching the other person's preferences.

We can use the metaphor of right and left brain as a useful shortcut for thinking about how to influence different preferences and in different organisational cultures or contexts. It's important to match preferences and to 'speak the same language'; this operates at the level of the individual as well as the organisation/culture. You can use the language of neuroscience to frame your reasoning when talking to CEOs about the power of storytelling and emotional intelligence. If you are more of a right-brain thinker yourself, develop your communication flexibility and adapt to the style of those you need to persuade.

2nd rule of influence:

When preparing to influence an audience to your cause, it's important to involve their heart as well as their mind so, alongside facts and intellect, share your emotions and tell a story. In business we often look to convince others by telling the *information* story, but if we want to influence we need to be better at telling the *inspiration* story.

What motivates us: fight–flight

Human beings are driven by two powerful forces: one pushing us forwards to approach something and one pulling us back to avoid something. We have strong tendencies to move toward or away from things. These two core motivations are the brain's most primitive survival mechanisms and are coded into our physiology and neurology. Broadly speaking, work converging from animal and human studies suggests that the left hemisphere of the brain supports approach behaviours while the right hemisphere is more concerned with withdrawal or avoidance behaviours. Approach and avoid behaviours are processed in separate hemispheres, it is believed, so that multiple approach and avoidance behaviours can be co-ordinated at one time and won't interfere with each other. Processing in these two hemispheres happens at multiple levels, some of which is conscious and some of which occurs so rapidly that we are not aware. Whether we are approach or avoid oriented seems to be linked to individual differences (personality traits), and this is linked to activity in the lateralised regions of the dorsolateral prefrontal cortex on the left and right side, respectively (see Fig. 1.2).

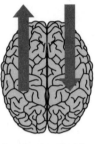

Approach   Avoid

FIGURE 1.2 The brain is structured for approach or avoid behaviours.

The brain's limbic system (sometimes known as the reptilian brain) is positioned at the top of the spinal column. From this position, it can rapidly send signals down the spinal column via long-range motor neurons to get us to move. Within the limbic system is the amygdala, an almond-shaped structure comprising multiple nuclei (groups of neurons) that acts as the brain's warning system (see Fig. 1.3). The right amygdala orients us to potential threat while the left amygdala is more concerned with ongoing threatening stimuli (a more sustained response to threat). For real emergencies and life-threatening situations, the low-level processing takes over and co-ordinated activity in the system cascades a series of instructions allowing us to move out of danger before we are even fully aware. Neurons in our motor cortex fire and make us move *before* the visual cortices in the occipital lobe have had time to process what our eyes have seen. So it's faster than sight.

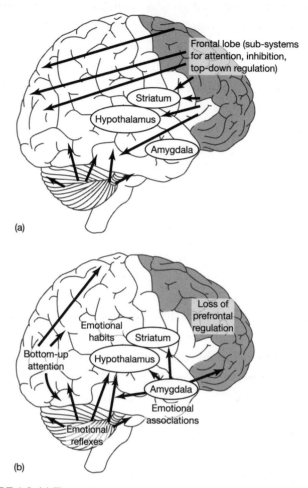

FIGURE 1.3 (a) The regions of the frontal cortex (subdivided into different cortices) are the seats of human reasoning, planning and top-down guidance of thinking and attention. When the frontal cortex is working well, we are able to regulate emotions and keep our attention on the task in hand. (b) The brain under stress. The pre-frontal lobe experiences reduced functioning as the limbic system hijacks attention. The hypothalamus, striatum and amygdala come on-line and are activated to prepare the body for fight or flight.

Source: Adapted from Arnsten, A F T (2009) Stress signalling pathways that impair prefrontal cortex structure and function, *Nature Reviews – Neuroscience*, 10, 410–422. Adapted by permission from Macmillan Publishers Ltd and Nature Publishing Group © 2009.

The amygdala also floods our body with the stress hormones adrenaline (short-term or acute threat) and cortisol (longer-term threats) that prime us for action. In conditions of acute stress, the sympathetic nervous system is activated via a sudden release of hormones (including adrenaline) which result in increased heart rate, accelerated breathing, sweating and blood pumping around the body preparing it for action (fighting or fleeing). This is why when we are really stressed and having a panic attack, it literally does feel like we are going to die as this primitive part of the brain is activated (and does not have the sophistication to know that there is not any real and actual danger to the individual).

In our modern world, the fight–flight response is often triggered inappropriately, particularly under conditions of chronic stress. While we no longer have to fight off predators, we do continue to experience social threats in the same way as we would a sabre-toothed tiger. Here are some of the common modern-day threats that trigger our fight–flight response:

→ having to meet unrealistic deadlines;
→ experiencing a lack of respect;
→ being treated unfairly;
→ not being appreciated;
→ feeling that you're not being listened to or heard.

If we continue to experience low-level amydgala hijacks at work, our capacity for creativity, problem-solving and decision-making are all reduced, which is why it's so important for managers and leaders to help to manage the brain states of employees. It is not possible for the body to stay in this hyped up state for long periods of time and soon the parasympathetic nervous system is activated to move us back into a more relaxed state. In this mode, creativity, problem-solving and decision-making skills are restored. Our fight–flight response is the most primitive and powerful emotional trigger we can experience and overrides rational thinking every time.

The US scientist, Adrian Raine, advises students in his criminal behaviour class to pretend to be asleep if they become aware of an intruder in their apartment because 90 per cent of the time thieves are only interested in grabbing what they want and running. Adrian was able to test out his own advice when holidaying in Turkey with his girlfriend when he woke to see an intruder standing above him in his bedroom in the middle of the night. Adrian said:

> *information from the senses reaches the amygdala twice as fast as it gets to the frontal lobe. So before my frontal cortex could rein back the amygdala's aggressive response, I'd already made a threatening move toward the burglar. This in turn immediately activated the intruder's fight–flight system. Unfortunately for me, his instinct to fight also kicked in. ... He hit me so hard on the head that I saw a streak of white light flash before my eyes.*

Even though Adrian had been giving this rational advice to his students for years his primitive limbic system overrode logic in a split second.

Source: Raine, A (2013) *The Anatomy of Violence*, pp. 3–4

The seven core emotions that drive behaviour

Emotions act as the brain's shortcut to guide our approach and avoidance behaviour. Although the brain codes experiences as 'good', 'bad' or 'neutral', there are seven core human emotions that are universally recognised regardless of culture or geography. These are happiness, sadness, fear, anger, disgust, contempt and surprise (see Fig. 1.4). These core emotions form the basis of our evolutionary journey from hunter gatherers to cyber-surfers and motivate us to either 'approach' or 'avoid' something in our environment. Sadness, fear, disgust and contempt are all 'away from' or avoid emotions, while anger can be either away from (withdrawal or stonewalling) or towards (aggression, criticism and derision).

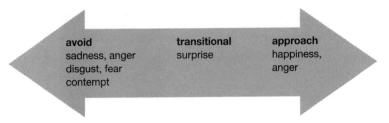

FIGURE 1.4 Core emotional motivators.

In his 2000 book *Integrative Neuroscience*, the neuroscientist, Evian Gordon, says that the brain's organising principle is to minimise danger and maximise reward, which means that everything we experience comes with an emotional 'tag' that is either good (toward) or bad (away from). Happiness is our only true 'toward' emotion while the emotion of surprise is a fleeting, transitional emotion until the moment we determine whether the surprise is pleasant or not. Surprise may be considered a type of emotional 'pause' as we gather further information to inform whether this is pleasant or unpleasant. These core emotions can be grouped into two distinct motivational drives; towards and away from. And when we think about influence, whether we want to sell a product or service, sell an idea or a social movement or inspire people to support a change, we need to be clear about how it will bring the audience closer to something they want (toward) or to avoid something they don't want (away from).

Every time you communicate to persuade somebody you need to be aware of these two primary motivations. Advertisers use these primary motivations all the time, from selling cars (toward: freedom, independence, comfort) to breath freshener (away from: social rejection).

What's their motivation?

The brain is designed to alert us to things that are threatening and has more circuits to detect threat than it does to detect reward. So we are predisposed to a more negative orientation because if we miss a threat we can die, whereas if we miss something more positive it will not kill us. This is a very simple but important idea for influence. The table below gives some reasons why, if we're not clear about how these human motivations work, we will fail to convince.

Toward message	Mismatch
A CEO announces a major change and develops an upbeat, positive message in the hope of getting everyone's support and buy-in.	Major change is experienced as a threat and the employees experience an emotional 'away from' reaction to the announcement. There is a disconnect between the speaker and audience.
You want to get your boss's support for an innovative new project and you focus on all the positive messages.	You fail to convince your boss because you do not take into consideration how you will manage risks and why your project should be chosen above others.

The science of emotions

Most of us like to believe that we make decisions based on our ability to weigh up logic and facts and, ultimately, to reason about our choices. Few of us like to believe we are predominantly influenced by emotion. Since Descartes famously stated '*I think therefore I am*', the role of the intellect has been esteemed and elevated with emotions often seen as less reliable guides for our choices. But in the last 20 years neuroscientists have been researching the role emotions play in dictating our choices about what we buy and who we vote for, and the decisions we make about our lives. And what they're discovering is that many of our decisions that we think are based on 'rational' thinking are in fact driven by often unconscious emotional responses.

Antonio Damasio's book *Descartes, Error* explored the role emotion plays in our ability to reason effectively. Damasio's research focused on the study of patients who suffered damage to the parts of the brain that affect decision-making and emotion. In one of his most famous experiments, Damasio worked with a patient called Elliot who had suffered frontal lobe damage affecting his emotional centres but leaving his intellectual capabilities intact. Damasio said:

> '(Elliot's) intelligent quotient (IQ) was in the superior range ...
> perceptual ability, past memory, short-term memory, new learning,
> language, and the ability to do arithmetic were intact' (p. 960) ...
> 'the tragedy of this otherwise healthy and intelligent man was that
> he was neither stupid nor ignorant, and yet he acted often as if he
> were. The machinery for his decision making was so flawed that
> he could no longer be an effective social being...' (p. 889).

Damasio was one of the first neuroscientists to explore brain areas related to emotional ability and the role this plays on our decision-making and the influence emotions have on our higher order cognitive functioning. His work shows that, in order to make effective decisions about our lives, we need to have feelings about them.

Since the publication of *Descartes, Error*, laboratories across the world have begun to turn their attention to the influence of emotion across a spectrum of research in order to understand more about human behaviour. It's this research that helps us understand the scientific basis for the role emotions play in persuading and influencing others. Think back to some important decisions you have made recently and complete the exercise below.

Exercise

Think about three important decisions you've made in the last year.

1. What criteria did you use to make the decision?
2. What was the balance between logical thinking and emotional input?
3. Have you ever put aside strong emotions to choose something on logic alone (perhaps to buy something you could afford rather than really loved)?

Where does emotional intelligence reside in the brain? A 2003 study by Reuven Bar-On *et al.* (exploring the neurological substrate of emotional and social intelligence) identified the specific brain centres that govern self-awareness, emotions and empathy: the amygdala, which is located in the midbrain is a neural hub for emotion; the somatosensory cortex helps us empathise with others; and the insula cortex makes us aware of our own body state and therefore helps us tune into others; the anterior cingulate helps us to control our impulses and handle strong emotions, and the prefrontal cortex, which is our brain's executive centre, helps us solve interpersonal problems, express our feelings and relate to others. This is illustrated in Fig. 1.5.

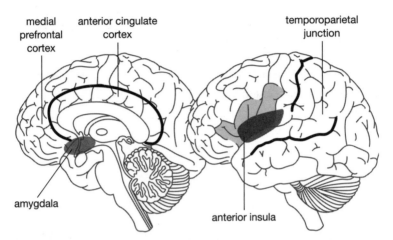

FIGURE 1.5 The regions of the social brain. Key regions include the amygdala, anterior cingulate cortex, medial prefrontal cortex, anterior insula and the temporoparietal junction. These regions together help us to make sense of the social world and understand the thoughts, feelings and behaviours of others.

Emotions are contagious

In one experiment, scientists brought together two strangers and asked them to sit silently in a room. Neither of the participants spoke, but within only two minutes, the most emotionally expressive person had managed to convey their emotions to the other person. Our brains transmit emotions to one another through chemical neurotransmitters in the brains of both people. We've developed an extraordinary capacity to pick up the subtle emotional cues and feelings of other people without us being consciously aware of it. Emotions are literally contagious.

A study carried out by Barsade in 2002 showed that when business school undergraduates participated in a leaderless group discussion with a confederate who was trained to manipulate their energy and pleasantness they were able to influence the group dynamic, showing that emotional contagion occurs in groups and that we are 'walking mood inductors', continuously influencing the mood, judgements and behaviours of others (Barsade, 2002, p. 666).

Barsade's model (see Fig. 1.6) shows how the energy and valence of a team member works at conscious and subconscious levels in the rest of the group to influence what happens in the team.

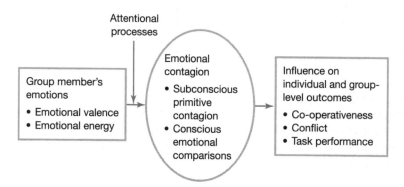

FIGURE 1.6 A model of group emotional contagion.

Source: Barsade, S G (2002) The ripple effect: emotional contagion and its influence on group B behaviour, *Administrative Science Quarterly*, 47, 644.

The research on emotional contagion shows how important your own emotional state is when you give that important presentation, that leaders can shift the emotions of employees during difficult times and that managers can raise team performance by managing their own emotional state. Preparing our emotional state is as important as preparing our content. We may need our IQ to help us put the deal together, but we need our EQ to close it.

Understanding others: mirror neurons

But it is not just about the message. In fact even more impor-tant – is about understanding your audience, whether that's an individual person you want to sell your idea to, your team, your boss or new customers you want to find for your busi-ness. It's also about your ability to create rapport, empathy and connection with others, and over the last 20 years, neu-roscience has been looking at the role our mirror neuron system plays in our ability to 'read' other people, to under-stand others' intentions and to pick up on others' emotions instinctively. Managing our own emotions and preparing our emotional state is just as important as preparing our message when we want to build relationships, empathy and rapport.

Brain plasticity

For most of the 20th century we believed the brain was unal-terable after a critical period in childhood, but neuroscience is now showing that the brain can change throughout our life and that both the physical structure and the physiology of the brain can be changed by our experiences. Every time we practise a new skill and every time we change our thinking, our habits and our responses we build new neural pathways that become more and more automatic. Learning the skills of influence is like learning any new skills; whether you want to be a more confident speaker, a more creative writer or a more inspiring leader of your business or community, it really is about developing opportunities to practise and hone your skills. The text introduces exercises that you can make part of your daily habits to help you strengthen and expand your toolkit for influence and persuasion.

The power of visualisation: set your goal

According to research, when we set a goal our brain creates an image as if we have *already* accomplished it because the brain can't distinguish between a *memory* of something that actually happened and an *image* of a future event. But what many of us discover is that it's easy to set a goal but not so easy to maintain our focus on the goal when we face setbacks and challenges. Soon we begin to experience self-doubt and anxiety and, unless we can deal with these, they can soon morph into full-blown fear. Fear affects our brain by shutting down our executive function and focusing our attention on a narrow field; getting away from whatever it is that threatens us. Fear extinguishes our creative and imaginative spark and blocks our brain from problem-solving and risk-taking. So the biggest barrier to achieving your goal is the fear you experience, not the challenge itself or the setbacks. All of these can be overcome. By understanding how fear shuts down the brain, we can practise something equally as powerful to help us stay focused and on track to achieve our goals, and that's the power of goal-setting and using the power of the mind to build new pathways to success.

Case study

Early research into the power of mental visualisation began in sports, and one of the most famous experiments was conducted by a Russian scientist who was asked to work with three different groups of Olympic athletes to find out whether the mind can cause the body to raise its performance and, if so, what was the optimum balance between mental and physical training. The first group of athletes were asked to spend 100 per cent of their time on physical training, the second group spent 75 per cent of their time on physical training and 25 per cent on mental training, the third group spent 50 per cent of their time on performing mental visualisation exercises and 50 per cent on physical training and the fourth group spent 75 per cent of their time on mental training and 25 per cent on physical training. It was the athletes in group four who spent 25 per cent of their time on physical training and 75 per cent on mental visualisation who had the highest performance results.

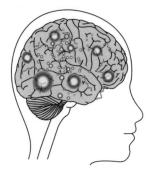

Use the power of your own mind to succeed.

Since the early research, mental visualisation has become standard practice for many sports people. Only recently, Wayne Rooney, the England striker, said in an interview:

> *Part of my preparation is I go and ask the kit man what colour we're wearing – if it's a red top, white shorts, white socks or black socks. Then I lie in bed the night before the game and visualise myself scoring goals or doing well. You're trying to put yourself in that moment and trying to prepare yourself, to have a 'memory' before the game.*

Sources: Mackay, H (2013) Mental training and visualization can help you live your dream, *South Florida Business Journal*, 18 January 2013 (http://www.bizjournals.com/southflorida/print-edition/2013/01/18/mental-training-and-visualization-can/html?page=all).
Jackson, J (2012) Wayne Rooney reveals visualisation forms important part of preparation, *The Guardian*, 17 May, 2012 (http://wwwtheguardian.com/football/2012/may/17/wayne-rooney-visualisation-preparation).

Influence in action

Influence doesn't really exist – the word itself is called a nominalisation (Chapter 4), which means that we take a verb (an action) and turn it into a noun (a thing). Influence is made up of a combination of different skills and abilities, such as being clear and concise about what you want to say, delivering your message with credibility and confidence, using persuasive language and being able to adapt when things don't go the way you want. So it will help to get clear about what specific skills you'd like to improve and in what situations you'd like to be more influential. Is it at work with your boss or colleagues? Do you need to be more influential as a manager with your team? Would you like to be able to sell your ideas to new customers? Or do you need to seek funding for a new project? Take some time to sit down quietly and write the answers to the following questions:

➡ Who do you want to influence?

➡ How will being more influential support you in your personal or professional life?

➡ In what contexts do you want to be more influential?

➡ In which situations are you already influential?

➡ How can you use what you already do well in one context and move it over to a new situation?

➡ Once you have more influence what will it do for you?

➡ What stops you from being more influential right now?

➡ If you could have three new skills or capabilities to help you be more influential, what would they be?

➡ Of these three, which one will give you the biggest benefit?

➡ What do you need to stay on track as you develop your skills of influence?

Once you set your goal you need to find ways to stay on track. Thoughts create images in the mind that kick-start a chain reaction of neural and chemical responses; when you think about something that is deeply upsetting you experience very different emotional and physiological responses in your body compared to when your thoughts are inspiring and encouraging. Our mind has a habit where one thought quickly leads to the next and the next in a 'themed' chain reaction – it's easy to find yourself going down very different emotional roads depending on how you think about something. If we experience a setback, our inner critic can be quick to make judgements: 'I knew they wouldn't like it'; 'I'm not smart enough or experienced enough or good enough'. Before we know it we begin to respond from the limbic brain which starts the fight–flight or freeze response; we become defensive, we want to run away and avoid the situation, or we feel stuck and anxious. But understanding about how our brain works can help us find ways to deal with these reactions.

Visualisation activates the brain to release a neurotransmitter called dopamine which is part of the brain's reward system and makes us feel good. While dopamine kick-starts our motivation, we need to maintain a steady dose to keep us on track when things get tough. Each time we visualise a compelling goal, our brain releases another dose of dopamine, so do what successful athletes do and make mental visualisation a regular part of your preparation – reimagine, reinvigorate and rebuild your goal, every step of the way – the more we practise anything, from playing the piano to goal-setting, the more it becomes wired into our brain circuitry.

Use words, pictures, feelings or sounds to give your brain a rich internal experience when focusing on your goal. Remember the golden rule of brain science; dopamine helps you stay on track and gives you a positive emotional boost.

Here are some daily practices that you can experiment with and see what works best for you.

→ **Daily diary:** at the start or end of each day spend five minutes writing about your goal. Make a note of everything you've done that day to move you closer towards achieving it. If you've experienced negative thoughts or emotions write about these. These thoughts come from a desire to protect ourselves and stay safe; treat them with compassion and acknowledge them as an important part of the process. They have no more or no less power than we give them.

→ **Mental visualisation:** take some quiet time and imagine yourself in the situations where you want to be more influential. See yourself there in full colour 3D technicolour, notice what you are wearing and feel the positive and powerful emotions that go along with your visualisation. You may like to hold a specific image in mind like a symbol, or you may like to direct your own internal movie that you can run in your mind whenever you have some quiet time.

If you are preparing to deliver a presentation, speech or stand in front of an audience, see yourself standing in front of them and watch them acknowledge you, thank you, praise you. If you are starting up in business imagine yourself receiving your first big order from an important customer. If you're going for a new job or wanting to sell your new project to your boss, imagine seeing their face smiling at you and thanking you for your great idea. Make your images multidimensional, colourful and emotional.

→ **Auditory goal-setting:** some people are very 'auditory' and are deeply drawn to sound. If that's you, choose a specific word or sentence that you can repeat to yourself. Write it down and speak or read the words every day. You might like to play a song that brings up powerful and positive emotional and mental associations while you imagine yourself achieving your goal.

➡ **Kinaesthetic:** pick the emotions that you want to experience when you are being your 'influential self' and go deeply inside them to notice their timbre, tone, shape or style. Wrap the emotion around you as if it's a warm, soft coat. Find a physical object you can use to remind yourself of your goal every time you touch it. Put it in your pocket, hold it in your hand, close your eyes and imagine yourself achieving your goal. Our brain records images, sounds and feelings in different areas and we each have different preferences for which sense is the most compelling for us – build a rich multisensory experience of your goal so that you build broad, deeper and lasting neural associations and pathways across all areas of your brain.

➡ **The morning pages:** Julia Cameron in her 1994 book, *The Artist's Way*, recommends doing a daily practice she calls 'the morning pages'. I've used this practice on and off for so many years and I find it helps me stay on track, work out what's blocking me, and helps me find other ways to get around it. Here are the instructions:

> Every morning, write three longhand pages of whatever comes into your head, it can be anything from deep insights to shopping lists. You can write about your dreams, your memories, your holiday plans, irritations, petty gripes – anything and everything that comes into your mind. Do not judge, just keep writing. It's not about thinking it all through and planning it, it's about letting it flow through from your mind to the page. Morning pages will help you in more ways than you know, try it for a month and see what happens.

➡ **Daily walks:** daily walking is a bit like the morning pages; there's something mysterious that happens when we are dealing with a problem or a challenge in our mind and we take it out for a walk. This is another practice that I do and can recommend, particularly if you are under stress. Exercise is proven to boost our self-esteem, mood and sleep quality and even to help us become more creative.

Brain Rules:

1. **Brain plasticity:** our daily habits of behaviour and thinking help to shape the brain's neural pathways.

2. **Mirror neurons:** we have a unique ability to understand and connect with others through our mirror neuron system. Tune in to others and use your emotions to build empathy and rapport.

3. **Exercise:** prepares the brain for peak performance.

4. **Visualisation:** the brain does not know the difference between what is imagined and what is 'real'. Use the power of the mind to code in success.

Top Tips:

1. Get clear about your intention – in which contexts do you want to be more influential?

2. Choose the skills that will help you get what you most want.

3. Practise a little and often.

4. Use successes and failure equally to hone your skills and reset your course.

Chapter 2

Influencing different personality styles

If there is any one secret of success, it lies in the ability to get the other person's point of view and see things from that person's angle as well as from your own.

Henry Ford

Outline

This chapter will help you understand how to influence through relationships by understanding different personality styles, and the power of emotions in influence.

1. How to thrive by understanding others
2. Same world – different views – understanding meta-programmes
3. Influence through your emotional state
4. Now I understand you, I can influence you
5. Mirror neurons – our two-way mirrors
6. Tune up your emotional awareness
7. How emotions drive behaviour
8. Tune in to others

How to thrive by understanding others

Six blind men in a village are told by the other villagers that there is an elephant coming to town. They have no idea what an elephant is, but they say to each other: 'Even though we are blind, we can still go to experience the elephant.' So they go together to the place where the elephant is kept and one by one, each begins to touch the elephant on a different part of its body.

'Hey, the elephant is a pillar,' said the first man who touched his leg.

'Oh, no! it is like a rope,' said the second man who touched the tail.

'Oh, no! it is like a thick branch of a tree,' said the third man who touched the trunk of the elephant.

'It is like a big hand fan' said the fourth man who touched the ear of the elephant.

'It is like a huge wall,' said the fifth man who touched the belly of the elephant.

'It is like a solid pipe,' Said the sixth man who touched the tusk of the elephant.

A wise man who is sighted tells the men that they are all right, and all wrong. They have each experienced only a single part of the elephant – but together they have experienced the whole elephant.

This story has been told to countless generations across different cultures to tell a simple truth; that we each see the world from our own perspective. We begin to build our worldview as children in our families, at school and in our social groups as we take on the core values, beliefs and attitudes of these communities of influence as effortlessly as breathing air; *Ah, this is the way it really is.* But the problem is that when we want to influence people who are 'not like us' (which will be often) our own blind spots can lead to us judge others and prevent us from developing the true skills of influence which are the ability to see the world from the other person's perspective and then build mutual respect and rapport. So what are some tools we can use when we need to prepare a communication, presentation or meeting with someone we want to influence? What are some top tips for helping us influence through relationship?

1st rule of influence through relationships:

See the world from the other person's perspective.

Same world – different views – understanding meta-programmes

We each have our own personal mental shortcuts to filter information, direct our attention and help us make decisions. These are called meta-programmes because they are unconscious cognitive habits that influence how we communicate and what motivates us.

Meta-programmes are keys to:

➡ How we like to be communicated with.

➡ Our strategies for decision-making.

➡ What motivates us to take action.

You can use meta-programmes to help shape your communication and influence others.

For example, we all have strategies for making decisions and choices; one person might spend weeks researching holiday resorts, prices and local attractions in order to choose their annual holiday while another person might pick a holiday on a whim, happy to turn up and see what happens. In terms of the meta-programmes, the first person would be making a decision based on a procedures meta-programme, while the second person would be making a decision based on an options meta-programme.

Once we understand other people's different preferences we can shape our communication and adapt our own relationship style to match more closely with theirs. This can make a huge difference in making sure we get our message heard and in meeting the other person's relationship values and preferences because we all naturally feel affinity and connection with people who 'match' us. Think about when somebody's tried to sell something to you or you met somebody new and there was a clash; it may well have been because you are each using different meta-programmes to communicate. Once we understand more about meta-programmes, we have a great tool to help us prepare our communication and adapt our own style to more closely match that of the other person.

Exercise

As you go through the meta-programmes below ask yourself the following questions:

1. What are your own preferences?

2. Do your preferences change in different contexts?

3. Have you experienced conflict with somebody because you have opposite styles?

4. How do you respond to someone who has the opposite style from you? Do you judge them as being 'wrong'?

5. How do you feel when you're with people who are the same as you?

Motivation: toward or away from

Some people are more motivated by what they want to move *toward* and some from what they want to move *away from*.

'Toward' people are often goal- and future-focused – always looking ahead at what they positively want to achieve. 'Away from' people are motivated by avoiding pain and reducing risk. They tend to focus on what they don't want and what they want to avoid. They value security and safety. And while we are all motivated to avoid pain and move towards pleasure, we each have slightly different 'set points' for these. Entrepreneurs, adventurers and risk-takers tend to be *toward* people. People who value security and certainty tend to be *away from* people. Businesses sell their products and services to consumers, and politicians sell to voters using both *toward* and *away from* messages; Nike's tagline 'Just Do It' is a *toward* message while political messages of 'austerity' and 'job losses' are *away from* messages. These two motivational forces operate at the level of action, cognition and emotion.

Tips for *toward* persuasion:

1. Talk about the positive emotions your offering gives (happiness, success, achievement, affection).
2. How will your offer increase, or give more of, what the person already has?
3. How will your offer improve something?
4. How will your offer increase something?
5. What future new possibilities will your offer help them achieve?

Tips for *away from* persuasion:

1. What negative emotions will this help avoid? (pain, loss, suffering, embarrassment, etc.)
2. How will it reduce what the person doesn't want? (danger, poor-quality results, poor performance)

Communication: big picture or detail

Some people like to be communicated with by being presented with the 'big picture' and some need to see the 'detail' in order to make a decision. A CEO who is a big picture thinker needs a compelling vision of what it is you're selling before getting to the detail, while the financial director may prefer the nuts and bolts before being convinced of your idea and will send you away unless you come fully prepared with the detail in hand. The CEO, on the other hand, may be much more comfortable to give you a green light to a great idea that they instinctively think might work and will be happy for you to gather the details and facts over time. Position your offering and present information to match the preferred style of your audience.

Tips for *big picture* selling:

1. Present your idea in a nutshell at the start. Big picture people want the elevator pitch – they want to see a compelling image or vision of a future state.

2. How will this get them to their end goal? Present information on a single page with the end goal in mind.

3. Use diagrams or images and summaries of the key benefits.

4. Talk about benefits and what this will help them achieve. Lead with the big picture and then follow up with detail if required.

Tips for *detail* persuasion:

1. Lead with the facts, figures and logic. Use detailed reports, background information and research. The detail provides feelings of assurance and security that you are fully in control of the information.

2. Remember that this meta-programme is often linked to an 'away from' programme where the person seeks to avoid risk and increase certainty.

3. Lead with the detail and then summarise with the big picture at the end.

Broadly speaking, holistic processing engages the right hemisphere while serial processing engages the more fine detail-loving left hemisphere (see Fig. 2.1). Holistic processing allows us to quickly scan information in order to get the gist while serial processing involves systematically scanning the information to then build an overall picture.

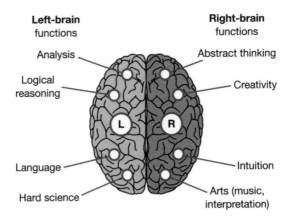

FIGURE 2.1 Present information to match the preferred style of your audience.

Decision-making: external or internal

Some people are very independent in their decision-making and rarely ask for other people's input or advice. They don't seek feedback from others because they know when they've done a good job (or bad job) because they are more *internally* referenced. Others, however, seek feedback, input and advice and will often need to get the opinion of others before making a decision. If you're a manager who is internally referenced but you have people in your team who are externally referenced, it's important to give them feedback and to recognise how important it is for them to feel motivated and acknowledged.

Tips for *externally* referenced persuasion:

1. Provide references, feedback and testimonials from others about your service or product.
2. Assume the person will need to consult with others before making a decision.
3. Provide detailed information for them to consult with others.

Tips for *internally* referenced persuasion:

1. Avoid using testimonials from other people (have them in your back pocket if necessary).
2. Present your ideas clearly and let the person know that you understand that it's their decision.
3. You might end the meeting by saying something like: 'Only you can decide what's best for you or your organisation.'

Decision-making: options or procedures

Some people like to be presented with options before making a decision while others want to see a step-by-step process that leads to a particular outcome. A good example of this meta-programme is when people go on holidays. Some people like to 'play it by ear', turn up in a new place and have no set agenda or plan, while others may have a detailed itinerary, will have booked accommodation months in advance and will want to stick to a set agenda. If you're a high options person and you've been on holiday with a strong procedures person, you will have experienced the challenges of negotiating with somebody who is your opposite style.

Tips for *options* persuasion:

1. Always present at least three options in your proposal or offer.

2. Build your proposal in a modular format so the person can choose different combinations.

3. Talk in the language of options: 'This solution may well be the best but let's have a look at several options.' Or: 'There are different ways that we can look at resolving this.' Or: 'We will make sure that we review progress along the way so that we can adapt and include additional options as we go.'

4. Provide flexibility in your offering.

5. Ask for their input and what they would like to see changed or added.

Tips for *procedures* persuasion:

1. Set out a logical step-by-step approach to your offer.

2. Show how you have come to a particular conclusion.

3. Present a timeline or plan that will give the person a structured approach.

4. Be clear about what will happen next, how it will work and how to deal with any problems.

Persuasion: task or relationship

Some people focus much more on the task at hand while others focus on the relationship between people. CEOs and senior leaders are often extremely task-focused in meetings or presentations and tend to spend much less time building and fostering relationships. You will mismatch this style if you are too chatty and appear over-friendly and informal when you come to sell your idea. On the other hand, if you go into a meeting with a person who values relationship over task and you don't take the time for small talk and social niceties you can appear abrupt and rude (in this case you are highly task-focused and they want to get to know you before deciding if they want to buy your idea). If you focus on relationship more and meet someone who is high task you might feel that they are uninterested and impolite.

Tips for *task-focused* persuasion:

1. Be prepared to get straight to the point and stick closely to your agenda.

2. Avoid small talk, be concise and be clear about any next steps and follow-up.

3. Make sure you arrive on time and are fully prepared.

Tips for *relationship-focused* persuasion:

1. Be prepared for the other person to lead the relationship more.

2. Be comfortable if they introduce small talk or ask you questions about yourself and want to get to know you before getting into the detail of the meeting.

3. Do some research on them so you can create more of a personal connection.

Kevin spent weeks meticulously preparing for an hour's meeting with Paul, a senior director, to get approval to proceed with a big project. Kevin wrote a 30-page report which included research findings, examples of best practice, financial analysis with a full budget and a comprehensive 12-month project plan. Kevin developed four different options at the bottom of the report and wanted to get Paul's input before proceeding to the next phase. He sent the report to Paul a week before to give him sufficient time to digest all the information.

When the day came for the meeting, Kevin received an email from Paul's secretary saying that he now had to fly to the US earlier and the meeting would only be 30 minutes. As soon as Kevin entered Paul's office, Paul said that while he'd not had time to read the report, he was looking forward to a short summary and hearing Kevin's top recommendations.

Kevin was completely unprepared for this, became flustered and began to notice feelings of anger and frustration. He'd spent months doing the research and wasn't sure himself which option Paul would support so he had no clear recommendation in his own mind. Kevin started to go through the detail which seemed to frustrate Paul. This reaction only raised the levels of stress and anxiety Kevin felt. Soon he began to waffle and felt overwhelmed and unsure of what exactly to say and how to get back on track. The rest of the meeting didn't go well and Paul ended it by agreeing to reschedule the meeting in a month's time when he would return from the States.

Paul was disappointed that Kevin was so unprepared and began to wonder if he was the right person to manage the project after all. Kevin felt deflated, embarrassed and angry and couldn't work out how the meeting had gone so wrong when he'd been preparing for it for weeks.

I've seen this story played out many times in business; in fact I've been on both sides. It's so easy to see the world from our own perspective and not be prepared for someone who will change tack, expect something else, not read the information we've sent and shorten the time they can offer us. Kevin's personal style is 'detail and relationship' and he assumed Paul would read the report and they would have an informal meeting to get to know one another more and discuss all the options. Paul is big picture and task driven and expected Kevin to recommend one solution which the finance director would review before final sign off.

So, before you step into the fray, stand in the other person's shoes, expect things to change, find out what they want from you and be prepared to flex your own style.

Meta-programmes: in a nutshell

Remember that meta-programmes are neither good nor bad – they are (mostly) unconscious preferences about the way we like to receive information, make decisions and choose between different options. When we are aware of our own and other people's preferences, we can collaborate better, play to our strengths and ensure we get the outcome we want.

2nd rule of influence through relationships:

Understand different communication styles, relationship values and decision-making strategies.

You can use meta-programmes to:

➡ Expand your understanding of other people's preferences.

➡ Influence decisions by matching communication style.

→ Influence decisions by matching decision-making style.

→ Influence decisions by adapting your relationship style to connect with and influence others.

Motivation style

Use this to think about what motivates the other person and then match your language and offering to that style.

→ Toward

→ Away from

Communication style

Use this to prepare your pitch, presentation or written documents. It's best to provide both big picture and detail but use this to decide what you *lead* with to start.

→ Big picture

→ Detail

Decision-making style

Use this to help you plan and prepare and then match your language and approach to influence decision-making.

→ Internal

→ External

→ Options

→ Procedures

Persuasion style

Use this to build rapport with the other person and match their relationship values.

→ Task

→ Relationship

Influencing others using meta-programmes

Meta-programme	Action
Toward *Motivation style*	Talk about goals, future vision, achievement, feelings of happiness, success, reward, aspiring, moving toward.
Away from *Motivation style*	Talk about avoiding pain, insecurity, managing risk, certainty, avoiding loss, what you don't want and what you want to move away from.
Big picture *Communication style*	Start with elevator pitch, story in a nutshell, compelling images of a future vision, use visuals, summaries, top line, key points. Move to detail last.
Detail *Communication style*	Start with brief objective but move quickly to provide detailed account. Bring in facts, figures, research, statistics and graphs. Focus on order and information. Move to the big picture and outcome last. Provide a summary and detailed report.
External *Decision style*	Set up a meeting where other people can join to make sure you include everyone who is part of the decision. Or say: 'I will come back to you once you've had time to consider and review.' Or, ask whether there are other people you might need to meet or talk to that would help them in their decision. Take your time and be prepared for several iterations. Bring in testimonials and feedback from others.
Internal *Decision style*	Language: 'Only you can decide.' Avoid relying on anybody else's opinion or feedback. Make it clear that you understand the final decision is theirs.
Task *Relationship style*	Be prepared to get straight to the point. Avoid small talk or asking personal questions. Be focused and organised and assume this will be the only meeting you will have. Let them do the talking. Be comfortable with silence. Be more formal in your overall approach and personal style.

▶

Meta-programme	Action
Relationship *Relationship style*	Let them lead. Be prepared to engage in small talk and focus on the relationship and building connection first before you get down to business. Relax and be more informal and conversational. Take your cues from them. Be prepared for the meeting to overrun so make sure you leave information with them if you haven't had time to cover it.
Options *Decision style*	Language: 'Here are several different options we can look at.' Prepare a modular approach to selling. Be flexible and creative in your approach. Come in with an open mind and be prepared to brainstorm alternatives with the person. High options people may have a preferred option that you don't know about. The key to this influencing style is to be flexible and adaptable.
Procedures *Decision style*	Language: 'Here's a detailed plan, with a step-by-step guide to share with you.' Bring in reports and facts and figures. Have a clear timeline and decision-making process laid out. Respect process.

So how do we know what someone's meta-programme is?

➡ For the communication meta-programme the easiest way is to ask people directly what they want when preparing for meetings, pitches and presentations. People will appreciate you considering how they like to receive information.

➡ For the relationship meta-programme, you may already be aware of this if you work closely with somebody or you can ask others to guide you on their preferred style. When meeting senior leaders assume they are task-focused (often because they will be under considerable pressure) and will appreciate a clear, succinct and well-prepared pitch that gets straight to the point. Avoid starting out with your company's credentials. You are at the meeting because you have already passed the test of suitability and time taken for you to talk about your credentials is time taken from understanding the other person's needs and presenting your ideas. Leave credentials in the back pocket (the last slide in the deck or at the back of the report) and assume that they are not necessary unless specifically asked for. Use every moment you have to connect, understand and listen to the other person.

➡ Get advice from others about what the person's preferred style is.

➡ People give us valuable information all the time about their preferences so make a habit of noticing.

Influence through your emotional state

The first place to start when we think about preparing to influence others is to get a deeper understanding of their personal preferences and motivators, and then understand how our own emotions affect and influence others.

> **3rd rule of influence through relationships:**
>
> Your emotional state is a powerful tool of influence.

If we mismatch at the level of personal connection and fail to create rapport, then it doesn't matter how well we've prepared our argument or material we will fail to convince and persuade. Influence is about the power of personal emotional connection. People really do buy 'people' more than they buy a 'logical' argument or proposition. And until recently we didn't really understand how this personal chemistry works between people. What the recent research in neuroscience has discovered is that there's a powerful neurological basis for empathy and emotional connection and, by understanding how this works, we can develop our own personal strategies for influencing – not through what we say, but through our own emotional state. But what is empathy anyway? And what does ice-cream have to do with the discovery of the neurological basis of empathy and rapport with others?

Case study

It was a hot summer day and a team of neuroscientists were working at a laboratory in Italy using neuro-imaging on the brain of a macaque monkey. During a lull in the experiment, one scientist took a break and went out to get an ice-cream. When he came back into the lab and moved his hand up to his mouth to lick the ice-cream, the motor cortex in the monkey's brain lit up at exactly the same time. This was not part of the experiment and the scientists were curious. Was the monkey's reaction a coincidence, or was something else happening? They repeated the action and got exactly the same result. They were intrigued. While none of the scientists in the room knew it at the time, they had just stumbled on one of the most important discoveries in brain science; the discovery of mirror neurons and the part they place in helping us learn through imitation. What we now know is that the mirror neurons that fired, deep in the monkey's motor cortex, enabled the monkey to neurologically perform *exactly* the same action at *exactly* the same time.

One of the leading neuroscience researchers, V S Ramachandran, in his 2011 work *The Tell-tale Brain: A Neuroscientist's Quest for What Makes Us Human*, proposes that around 75 000 years ago humans took a major evolutionary step when our brains developed a more sophisticated mirror neuron system. For the first time, our ancestors could adopt the point of view of another person; they could watch an animal being skinned, somebody light a fire or build shelter and create an 'internal simulation' of the action. This new brain circuitry accelerated our ability to learn and share critical skills of survival and safety such as fire and shelter making.

But, while some of our mirror neurons are specialised to mirror other people's motor skills, there are a smaller percentage of mirror neurons (around 10–20 per cent) in our somatosensory cortex, the inferior parietal cortex and the anterior insula regions that fire when we see somebody else being touched. This may be related to our ability to make sense of someone else's internal emotional landscape. Activation of these mirror neurons allows us to 'read' and tune in to the emotional states of others and, from this, form the basis of our ability to empathise, understand another person's point of view and build rapport with others. Our ability for rapport is not just a cognitive thinking process but is in fact a deeply hardwired brain activity.

Now I understand you, I can influence you

The discovery of mirror neurons that day in the monkey's brain opened up new areas of research including a new field of neuroscience called *interpersonal neurobiology* which explores how two brains, in two bodies interact. It's all about our brain-to-brain connections; how one person's thinking, emotional state and the words they use can affect another person at the level of their neurology. It's the insula in the brain which acts as our emotional barometer and helps us recognise the emotions that pass across somebody's face.

Case study

A group of scientists set up an experiment to understand how emotional contagion operates. They put two people in a room together and asked them to maintain eye contact for two silent minutes. At the start and end of the experiment participants were asked to complete a mood checklist. What the scientists discovered was that the person who was the most emotionally expressive of the pair was able to transmit their emotions to the other person. In other words, the person with the most powerful emotional state was able to shift the other person's emotional state in only two minutes.

Source: Goleman, D, Happy or sad, a mood can prove contagious, *The New York Times*, 15 October 1991 (http://www.nytimes.com/1991/10/15/science/happy-or-sad-a-mood-can-prove-contagious.html?pagewanted=all&src=pm).

Interpersonal neurobiology is one of the most exciting branches of neuroscience for anyone interested in how we communicate and influence others. We might think we are in private worlds where our thoughts and emotions are discreet and 'hidden' from view, but in fact our emotional state is a powerful tool of influence. If you see a look of fear pass across somebody's face your mirror neurons fire and your brain creates an internal 'map' of that same emotion in your insula so that you can 'understand' the intentions and emotion of the other person. This momentary emotional mirroring allows you to respond, react and reassure (or if you are not in tune with the other person to miss the emotional information entirely). As Dan Siegel says in *Mindsight*: '*I've come to call this set of circuits – from mirror neurons to sub cortical regions, back up to the middle prefrontal areas – the "resonant circuits." This is the pathway that connects us to one another.*' (2011, p. 61). So influence is not only about tuning in to other people and how they are feeling in order to respond and adapt how you sell, but also how you manage your emotional state and its effect on others.

Mirror neurons – our two-way mirrors

But what's critical in the field of influence is that our mirror neuron system operates as a two-way feedback loop. When we are exposed to powerful negative emotions such as fear and anxiety, these can pull us into an emotional downward spiral (think about how quickly fear can spread through a group). We can also share in the positive emotional states of groups; think about being at a sporting event when your team is winning or at a concert when the crowd is singing in unison – emotions spread quickly and can shift others into an upward emotional spiral. And this two-way emotional feedback loop operates in every context: in groups, in one-to-ones and at work.

When we want to influence the outcome with other people our emotional state is really our secret weapon because it has a profound effect on how other people feel about us, how much information they can take in (because if they are anxious they will find it hard to concentrate) and whether we are able to build rapport with others. Let's look at how the mirror neuron system can operate in different contexts as both a negative and positive influence.

> **4th rule of influence through relationships:**
>
> The mirror neuron system allows us to resonate emotionally with others and affects every interaction we have.

Mirror neurons as a negative two-way mechanism in influencing others

Context	Effect
A CEO delivers a presentation to employees about a major change and restructure that will cause job losses and upheaval in the business. The CEO is matter-of-fact, 'logical' and rational in an attempt to contain employees' feelings of anxiety. The CEO feels anxious and nervous about how the audience will respond so chooses to be even more 'distant' and formal than he normally is. **Mirror neurons**: feelings of anxiety and discomfort.	Employees feel threatened and insecure. Their brains will find it difficult to focus on facts and details because they will be thinking about their own survival. The CEO's style and delivery as well as his feelings of anxiety come across as cold and uncaring. Employees feel unimportant and 'dispensable'. **Mirror neurons**: heightened feelings of fear, anxiety, insecurity and uncertainty.
A manager is under considerable stress and pressure to deliver an important project. She becomes increasingly irritable, short-tempered and demanding of her team members who are important in helping her achieve her target. **Mirror neurons**: feelings of anxiety, fear, insecurity, anger and a need to control.	Her team begins to dread it when she's in the office. They become increasingly anxious about 'getting it wrong' and begin to withdraw and avoid her, which only increases her feelings of anxiety and being 'out of control'. **Mirror neurons**: feelings of fear, anxiety and frustration. The team may end up wanting to withdraw their support.

▶

You are presenting to a new client and, while you have a great PowerPoint deck and all of your information prepared, you are in a state of extreme fear and anxiety and your nerves take over: you avoid eye contact, look down at the ground and speak quickly in order to get to the finish line as quickly as possible. **Mirror neurons**: feelings of terror, fear and embarrassment.	The people you are pitching to want you to do well but become increasingly uncomfortable and anxious themselves as they pick up on your powerful toxic emotional state. Your audience find it difficult to listen to what you're saying. **Mirror neurons**: feelings of anxiety that often end up in feelings of being angry and wanting to literally 'get away' from you.

We often focus on the 'content' of our message, particularly when we need to have a difficult conversation or to deliver a difficult message. But these are the most important times to focus on managing the emotional response of our audience, specifically by thinking about how *your* emotional state impacts on the group. When people are anxious or in fear (of say losing their jobs or dealing with a major change) they can move quickly into fight or flight response which will shut down their capacity to hear your message, so it's important to move people back into a more receptive state of mind. Now let's take a look at how we can turn this around to positively influence others and achieve our outcome.

Mirror neurons as a positive two-way mechanism in influencing others

Context	Effect
A CEO delivers a presentation to employees about a major change and restructure that will cause job losses and upheaval in the business. The CEO adopts an informal, conversational style and talks from the heart, without notes or PowerPoint slides. He talks about his own feelings of loss and disappointment and reassures employees about the way the change will be handled. The CEO is able to handle his own emotions in order to focus on the emotions of employees. **Mirror neurons**: feelings of understanding and empathy.	Employees feel threatened and insecure. The CEO's more informal style as well as his ability to share his feelings help to reassure employees that they are important. **Emotions**: reduced feelings of fear and insecurity, increased feelings of being acknowledged.
A manager is under considerable stress and pressure to deliver an important project. She talks to her team about the demanding deadlines and finds ways to manage her own stress and to ask for her team's help and support to deliver the project. She acknowledges, appreciates and recognises the contribution of team members. **Mirror neurons**: feelings of anxiety, but these are reduced through the reassurance and support of her team. Camaraderie and team spirit.	Her team feel more motivated to support her because they understand the consequences and feel needed and important. Appreciation and recognition help to raise their commitment and desire to contribute. **Emotions**: feelings of safety and security (even when times are hard we are safe from criticism and can pull together). Feelings of pride and achievement.

▶

You are presenting to a new client. You have a great PowerPoint deck and all of your information prepared. You are in a state of anxiety, but you spend a lot of time preparing your emotional state to control this as much as you can. You decide to let people know you are a little nervous. **Mirror neurons**: feelings of anxiety as well as excitement and anticipation.	The people you are pitching to want you to do well and are able to concentrate on your message because they are relaxed and at ease. The audience empathise with you when you share your genuine anxiety and their empathy helps to reassure and relax you a little more. **Emotions**: feelings of anticipation and interest in what you have to offer and share. Feelings of empathy as you come across as authentic and open.

The dance of rapport

Our ability to accurately read and respond to other's emotions as well as maintain a positive emotional state when we need to is a critical building block in our ability to influence them. Persuasive communicators tune in to their audience, they notice if they are energised, attentive and motivated and, if not, they adjust, adapt and respond to get things back on track. We match the listener's emotional state and monitor and modulate our own emotions in a way that allows the listener to feel safe and contained. In this low-threat environment, thinking and creativity can thrive.

If you are an interviewer, leader or sales person who is *tuned out* to others you will soon be having an emotional one-way monologue. But when you are able to pick up the cues that others unconsciously send out, whether through their tone of voice or body language, you will quickly build rapport and you will have the ability to emotionally *dance* with the other person.

Tune up your emotional awareness

Tune up your own emotions and set your own emotional compass when you want to influence others. Your emotional state is communicated all the time and influences those around you. The first building block is to develop your own awareness of your emotional state. How quickly can your mood be shifted from positive to negative or vice versa? Are you the leader in the neural dance with others or are you a follower? Do you help to lift and shift the mood of others to a more productive and open state? Or are you more of a follower and quickly feel affected by other people's moods? When you notice you are in a negative or bad mood how long do you stay there? Do you have strategies to help you recover and become more positive?

The STAR model

Use the STAR model to help you build your emotional awareness, emotional resilience and move back into positive emotions so you can positively influence others:

Switch

There are many things that switch our emotions from positive to negative: the train being cancelled when we're already running late for an important meeting; an urgent email from our boss saying they want to see us without letting us know why; a friend cancelling on us at the last moment. Before we know it we can start to feel angry, irritated or anxious. These emotions in turn affect our physiology as our brain releases cortisol and adrenaline into our bloodstream. We experience tension in our body, butterflies in our stomach, our jaw clenches and we rapidly move to a stressed state.

Thoughts

As soon as we notice our emotions change we need to become aware of how our thoughts change in response to them. We all have what's known as 'self-talk' where we hold an internal one-way dialogue in our mind and say things like: 'I knew it. This always happens to me, it's just typical when something's really important things always go wrong.' Or, 'It's going to be a disaster. They'll be so angry at me for being late.' Or, 'I'm in trouble. I wonder what I've missed or done wrong?' Or, 'My friend is so inconsiderate, why do people always let me down?' And one thought leads to another and starts a chain reaction of negative thinking and mental catastrophising. Our thoughts create increasingly negative emotions and reactions, stress pushes us into fight–flight or freeze mode and further prevents us from thinking clearly and responding appropriately, and this becomes a vicious circle as we travel further and further down the emotional low road.

Assess, argue and analyse

Once we become aware of how we are beginning to think about the situation we can begin to assess what's really going on, analyse our thinking and argue the other side of case.

'Trains are often late, it's not personal to me and I really didn't build in enough time for anything to go wrong. I need to calm down so I can work out what's best to do.' Or, 'I really don't know what my boss wants to see me about, so there's no point in imagining the worst case scenario. Perhaps she has an important project she wants to me to do?' Or, 'My friend really does care about me, she's often been there for me when I've needed her and it's important for me to be able to let her off the hook this time and not make her feel guilty.'

Restore, resolve and reset

Once we can see how quickly our thinking becomes part of the problem, we can start to reset our emotional state by changing our thoughts. The truth is that no matter what happens, panic, stress, negative thinking and negative emotions only add fuel to the fire. So we need to use our executive brain function (our intelligence and logic) to understand how to move back to a more resourceful state and then we need to reset our emotional state.

Exercise

Make the STAR process work for you by making it a strong mental habit. Practise it to strengthen your emotional resilience.

Manage your emotional triggers

Here are some other daily practices to help you manage your emotional triggers.

Use your body to shift your emotions

Exercise is proven to benefit our brain as well as our mood and can help us shift our emotional setpoint and get us back into balance. Exercise has been shown to have positive effects on our brain through neurogenesis (developing new neurons) and to lift our mood by releasing endorphins which releases feel-good hormones (McGovern, 2005, The effects of exercise on the brain). Walking is a great exercise when you want to 'mull things over' – there's a kind of magic that happens after around 10–15 minutes when your mind becomes more open to making new and more creative connections. Walking increases the amount of oxygen and glucose that is sent to your brain, which helps you reduce stress, improve concentration and improve memory function, all of which help you find new insights and solutions to any challenges you're facing.

Write a journal to shift your emotions

Another proven strategy is to keep a daily journal and note the emotions you experience in a day. Notice what triggers your emotions; is it what somebody said, their tone of voice or body language? Think about the conclusions you come to, it's often not so much *what* happened but how we interpret it which can lead us to negative or self-defeating thoughts. Writing will help you challenge your thoughts, help you develop new ways of seeing things and build your emotional resilience.

Case study

Matthew Lieberman, a psychologist who works at the University of California in LA and researches the effect of writing on our brains, found that the act of writing helps to calm the amygdala (which is connected to our fight–flight response). Volunteers underwent brain scans and scientists found that those who wrote things down matched the brain scans of the volunteers who were consciously trying to control their emotions. Lieberman said: *'Writing seems to help the brain regulate emotion unintentionally.'* If you make this a daily practice for a month you will have created a habit which is much easier to sustain.

Source: Sample, I, Keeping a diary makes you happier, *The Guardian*, 15 February 2009 (http://www.theguardian.com/science/2009/feb/15/psychology-usa).

Mindfulness

Another powerful strategy to help you manage your emotions and build emotional resilience, empathy and insight is to practise mindfulness. Mindfulness training increases our ability to choose where to focus our attention, and this ability is most important when the emotional brain is hijacking our attention. When we are stressed and under pressure, the emotional systems of the brain take over and our ability to think creatively and problem solve is reduced. Mindfulness training allows us to accept and absorb even strong negative emotions and then then redirect our attention to where we want it to be.

A key aspect of mindfulness training involves the repeated bringing of attention to the body and bodily sensations. This has a two-fold benefit. Firstly, it allows us to learn more about our own personal body signature of emotions – we become more sensitive to emotional changes and better able to deal with strong emotions. Secondly, paying attention to the body allows us to be in the 'present moment'. This is the antidote to the tendency of the stressed and anxious mind.

There is now four decades of research on mindfulness training showing that it can improve emotional and cognitive functioning and that these changes arise as a result of changes in the structure and function of the brain. Further to these findings, mindfulness training is now being applied in a variety of sectors including business, education and health.

How emotions drive behaviour

Banking, more than many other industries, embodies the principles of logic, rationality and hard facts; mathematicians, economists, statisticians and even rocket scientists are employed by banks to boost their intellectual firepower. You could say that banks exemplify 'left brain' thinking but, following the financial crash in 2008, it's become clear that powerful emotions such as greed and fear played a significant part in decision-making by traders, risk officers, regulators, CEOs and ratings agencies. The dominant organisational emotions are conveyed by the top leaders and cascade down via the mirror neuron system throughout the organisation.

Case study

A study by Diana Robertson and Andrew Bate of the Wharton School showed that it was managers who demonstrated high levels of emotional intelligence who outstripped their peers when it came to all-round strategic thinking. The research measured the brain activity of managers on an executive MBA programme while reacting to fictional business dilemmas. The best performers were those who showed more neural activity in the brain areas associated with empathy and emotional intelligence – the insular, the anterior cingulate cortex and the superior temporal sulcus. These managers were able to balance IQ and EQ better and to take into account the impact a major strategic change would have on the employees that would have to implement the change.

Source: Gilkey, R *et al.* (2012) When emotional reasoning trumps IQ.

Source: Dr Tamara Russell

In the past we focused more on intelligence but, over the last 20 years, we've become increasingly aware of the important role emotion plays in leadership and in positively influencing others.

Tune in to others

The next step is to tune in to the emotions of others and you can do this by 'standing in their shoes'. Ask yourself the following questions to help you uncover what the world looks like to other people:

➡ What's most important to this person?

➡ What are their values?

➡ What motivates them?

➡ What are they afraid of?

➡ How do they feel about this particular issue?

➡ How do they see you?

Tips for leaders:

1. Leaders play a critical role in managing the emotions and motivation of others.

2. People look to the leader of a group, team or organisation for reassurance and clarity when there is a threat to the group or a challenge to be faced.

---

3. The emotions of leaders help shape the culture and level of performance in the organisation (people underperform when they experience fear, anxiety or insecurity).

4. Leaders can use emotional energy to inspire, motivate and direct others.

5. Businesses, groups and teams need positive emotional energy to flourish.

The skills of empathy

There are three skills of empathy that will help you be influential at managing others.

Cognitive empathy

This means understanding how the other person sees things and understanding their perspective. Even if you need to say no to a project or an idea, make time for the other person to fully present their idea; it's much easier to accept a decision when it's been fully explored and acknowledged. Take the time to encourage the person to acknowledge the good ideas and the work involved.

Emotional empathy

Notice, acknowledge and respond to the emotions of people in your team to build rapport. Notice when the team is under stress and create opportunities for people to move back into a calm state of mind. Create social opportunities for people to express and share their feelings as well as celebrate and publicly acknowledge achievements to create feelings of pride, achievement and recognition.

Empathetic concern

Notice when somebody needs your help or support, when they're under pressure or missing deadlines. Provide advice and counsel. Listen with deep attention and ask incisive questions to help somebody think through a problem and come up with their own solutions. This is the role of the coach–manager who uses their own emotions intelligently to develop the next generation of leaders.

Giving feedback

When managing other people make sure you give positive praise and feedback and empathise with others. Researchers found that if we give negative feedback in an empathetic and positive way people are still able to maintain a positive emotional state and feel good about themselves, whereas, if we give the same feedback to the person in a critical and cold tone they come out feeling negative. The content of our message is exactly the same, but a positive tone and style is what people remember and will help them assimilate and act on the information. When people feel criticised their brain moves quickly into fight–flight and they are more likely to become defensive and tune out your message.

Brain Rules:

1. The brain has an open loop system and emotional states are communicated through the mirror neuron system.
2. The person with the strongest emotional state has the biggest influence.
3. Leaders play an important role in the emotional regulation of others.

4. When we meet people's emotional needs they experience connection and empathy with us which allows us to influence.

5. Fear blocks our ability to influence because it shifts people into fight–flight response.

6. Smiling changes our brain chemistry by releasing neuropeptides, dopamine, endorphins and serotonin which help us fight stress, lower our heart rate and blood pressure and lift our mood.

7. Smiling is contagious so is a simple but powerful way to connect, reassure and then influence.

Top Tips:

1. Tune up your own emotions to positively influence others. Build your emotional awareness and emotional resilience.

2. Prepare your emotional state with as much care as your message whenever you want to influence others.

3. Emotion is persuasive not logic or facts – support your message with emotional motivators.

4. People move away from pain and toward pleasure; use these core motivating forces to influence.

5. Emotions change the world.

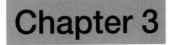

Chapter 3

We're all talking but nobody's listening

Attention is an act of creation. Listening to reply is different from listening to ignite. As the thinker, knowing you will not be interrupted frees you to truly think for yourself.

Nancy Kline (2009) *More Time to Think,* **p. 33.**

Outline

This chapter will tell you why listening is one of the most underrated but important skills of influence and give you practical tips to practise your listening skills.

1. Listening – the hidden skill of influence

2. Are you listening?

3. What neuroscience can teach us about listening

4. The deadly habits of poor listening

5. The power of deep listening

6. Listen out and listen in

7. How can we encourage others to listen?

8. What leaders can learn about the art of listening

9. The hidden power of questions

Listening – the hidden skill of influence

If you had to choose a single skill that would guarantee the gift of influence, what would you choose? Would it be the skill of a confident presenter; someone who can stand in front of a large group and entertain and persuade? Would it be the skill of a wordsmith; someone who can shape language and tell a story that connects with an audience? Or would it be the skill of a great listener; someone who is able to maintain deep and focused attention? In our quest for influence we are often attracted to those skills that appear to be of greatest value; the public profile of the speaker or writer. These are both important skills in our toolkit, but the greatest gift of all is often what appears to be most ordinary and least difficult. If you become a master at the other skills but fail to build your skill as a listener, the other skills will be largely wasted. You may come across as someone who has knowledge, who's confident and a good communicator, but you won't have true influence. The art of listening is what truly influential people do. It's what makes them great.

Remember – listening is a radical act in a world that loves to talk.

Case study

Ex US President Bill Clinton is renowned for his personal charisma and ability to make everyone he meets feel as if they are the only person in the room. It's a powerful tool of influence and, like President Obama, Clinton has been practising the skill of deep listening much of his life. As Ken Aulett described in his story from the *Spokane Chronicle* in 1992, he never forgot the first time he noticed Bill Clinton. Clinton was attending a National Governors' conference in 1986 where six mothers had been invited to describe their experiences of life on welfare. It was abundantly clear from Clinton's responses that unlike many of those present he had listened carefully to what the women said and taken in the detail. He addressed them by name and was able to recall their stories, asking questions and making policy suggestions based on what they described.

Anyone who spent time with Bill Clinton on the campaign trail could see that he was a great listener with a knack of drawing people from all walks of life out and encouraging them to talk. He had an ability to translate these conversations into speeches which truly connected with his audience.

Source: Aulett, K, Best presidents are good listeners, and that gives Clinton advantage, *Spokane Chronicle*, 16 July 1992 (http://news.google.com/ newspapers?nid=1345&dat=19920716&id=ZFlYAAAAIBAJ&sjid=AfoDAAAAIB AJ&pg=4961,2146467).

In the toolkit of influence, the art of listening is *the* most influential skill of them all – listening is the foundation upon which every other skill depends. Because if you don't *really* listen, you're likely to miss the important information from your team, your employees, your colleagues and your friends. Yet when you ask most people what they want in order to become more influential they say: 'I want to be taken more seriously.' Or, 'I want them to listen to me.' Or, 'I want to be credible and confident when presenting.' Nobody ever says they want to become a better listener because it's hard to believe that by not talking we are more persuasive and influential. We grow up believing that we need to have opinions; to become more knowledgeable and expert so people will listen to us. As we progress in our careers we're expected to have more to say, not less. We feel we need to have the answers, not keep asking questions. And the more senior you are, the more people listen to you – not the other way around. Being listened to is a mark of status and respect. In business meetings, it's the senior people that get the lion's share of the floor. So the very idea of saying less, of sitting back and observing and listening seems counter-intuitive as a way to increase influence. What if somebody else gets in before you? What if they have the great idea first? In a world full of speakers, listening can just feel like you've given up the race.

> **1st rule of influence through listening:**
>
> Listening will help you find out what you really need to know.

Are you listening?

Have you heard these phrases recently: 'You're not hearing me.' Or, 'That's not what I said.' Or, 'You're missing the point.' And if you're a leader or manager have you heard employees say 'They don't care what we think.' Or, 'They don't want to know what's really going on.' If you have, then chances are you may be in the habit of hearing without really listening. Or perhaps you're on the receiving end? When was the last time somebody remained silent even after you stopped talking because they noticed you were still thinking? How do you feel when other people jump in before you've finished your sentence? Or they look around the room or check their phone message while you're speaking? How many meetings have you been to where most people in the room are looking everywhere else, but at the speaker?

On average, we listen to each other for *eight seconds* before we either interrupt or actively stop listening. Eight seconds. That's not enough time to boil a kettle. Interrupting is not only butting in, it starts the moment the voice in our head starts to rehearse our answer, or search for similar anecdotes or for the perfect bit of advice. Then we wait for the smallest of gaps in the conversation – an in-breath, a moment of silence, a pause, a look to the side – and then we jump in and off we go. It's a habit most of us are not even aware of. We think we're listening when all we're doing is waiting to speak. So the first thing to do is to find out how good a listener you are and then practise turning up your attention dial and your power to influence through deep attention.

Exercise

Using these techniques test your listening skills

1. The next time you have a conversation with someone (today), notice how long you remain totally focused on what the other person is saying.

2. As soon as you notice a thought, judgement or you begin to form your response, make a note of how long you were able to listen.

3. Repeat the exercise three times a day for a week. At the end of the week make a note of the longest time you remained focused on the other person.

4. How difficult did you find the exercise? What thoughts pop into your mind when listening to others?

Use these techniques to test other people's listening skills.

1. The next time you have a conversation, notice the moment the other person withdraws their attention from you.

2. Make a mental note of how long you were given the gift of attention.

3. Do this three times a day for a week and then find out who's the best listener you know.

4. How does it feel when you are really listened to?

5. How does it feel when people interrupt?

2nd rule of influence through listening:

Start by finding out how well you really listen.

What neuroscience can teach us about listening

Hearing has evolved as our primary alarm system because it operates out of sight and works even when you're asleep. The auditory system is like a volume control and filters out sounds that you don't need to pay attention to. But if we hear a sudden noise our 'startle response' system warns us about any danger that occurs outside awareness. We have what neuroscientists call 'bottom-up' and 'top-down' attention. Bottom-up attention is when we hear something that intrudes, like hearing our name spoken by somebody on the other side of the room, while top-down attention is where we consciously choose to pay attention to what we're hearing.

The temporal lobe (Fig. 3.1a) is responsible for automatic hearing and for recognising patterns in sound waves so that we can process sound into language. We engage our frontal lobe (Fig. 3.1b) when we begin to pay conscious attention and our limbic system when we tune into the deeper level of meaning – emotional content, tone and nuance, body language, energy and emotional state in others. Deep attention takes a significant amount of cognitive effort and so requires us to engage the limbic system (Fig. 3.1c). We need to practise if we are to become deep listeners.

(a) Temporal lobe: hearing
Automatic
Pattern recognition
Sound waves become words

(b) Frontal lobe: paying attention
Monitor speech
Make judgements
Create meaning linked to our own
experiences and memories

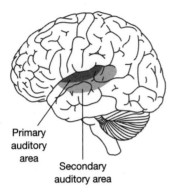

Primary
auditory
area
Secondary
auditory area

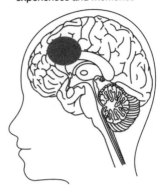

(c) Limbic system: deep listening
Pay attention
Notice emotional content of
speech, voice tone, nuance

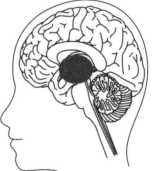

FIGURE 3.1 The primary level of processing is the auditory cortex, which then feeds information to the secondary auditory cortex and then on into the brain for further processing (interpretation, links with memory, imagery, etc.).

Hearing is easy, it's automatic, we can't turn it off, but using top-down attention is hard when distractions are leaping into our ears every fifty-thousandth of a second. For an untrained mind, it is easy to be distracted by sounds, sights and other distractions such as telephones ringing and email 'pings'. It can take a lot of brain energy to re-focus our thoughts as we experience multiple distractions. We might believe that we can work or listen while doing other things, or that we can 'half' listen, but our brains just don't work like that.

Case study

The scientist Harold Pashler showed that when people do two cognitive tasks at once, their cognitive capacity can drop from that of a Harvard MBA to that of an eight-year-old. It's a phenomenon called *dual task interference*. In one experiment, Pashler had volunteers press one of two keys on a pad in response to whether a light flashed on the left or right side of a window. One group only did this task over and over. Another group had to define the colour of an object at the same time, choosing from among three colours. These are simple variables – left or right, and only three colours – and yet doing two tasks took twice as long, leading to no time saving. This finding held up whether the experiment involved sight or sound, and no matter how much participants practised. If it didn't matter whether they got the answer right, they could go faster. The lesson is clear: if accuracy is important, don't divide your attention.

Source: Pashler, H (1994) Dual-task interference in simple tasks: data and theory.

3rd rule of influence through listening:

There's a big difference between hearing and listening. Listening requires focused attention.

The deadly habits of poor listening

There are many reasons why we might hear what's being said but fail to listen – here are the most common ones:

→ **We don't practise**: Listening is like any skill, it requires practice. Most of us have spent our lives interrupting, jumping in, losing attention and letting our thoughts wander.

→ **We don't value it as a skill**: Businesses place greater emphasis on the skills of talking, presenting, knowing, advising, telling, consulting and selling. It's little wonder that listening seems like the poor cousin of these communication skills. There are few businesses that teach listening skills in leadership training.

→ **We're impatient**: We find it hard to sit still and stay open to the other person. If we're under stress the brain operates under par and we can find it difficult to give somebody our full attention.

→ **The voice in our head**: It's not possible to listen to somebody else at the same time as listening to the voice in our head – our own thinking drowns out our ability to pay attention to what the other person is saying.

→ **We judge**: We think we know where the other person's thinking is going and stop really listening.

→ **Distractions**: In this world of open plan offices, telephones, 'always-on' social media, the ringing of mobile phones, emails, sound bites, banter and the thousands of background sounds that interrupt us all day, we often find ourselves holding conversations and meetings while being assaulted by endless and constant auditory distractions. Turning down our 'bottom-up' attention and turning up our 'top-down' attention requires discipline and effort.

→ **We're afraid of what we might hear:** Sometimes we think it's just easier not to find out. Listening might mean we need to change tack, reverse a decision, feel less certain or expose ourselves to being challenged.

The power of deep listening

So how can listening become a tool of influence? Nancy Kline is a pioneer in encouraging deep thinking to improve the quality of our lives, schools and workplaces. In her 2009 book, *More Time to Think*, she says, '*The quality of everything human beings do, everything – everything – depends on the quality of the **thinking** we do first*' (p. 16). Since 1973, Nancy Kline has been exploring what conditions enable people to do their best thinking and has developed what she calls 'The Thinking Environment' which comprises ten core components, one of which is the skill of listening:

> *If you give attention of generative quality, born of deep interest in what the person thinks and will say next, they will think better around you than they will if you interrupt them or listen only in order to reply* (p. 31). *Attention is an act of creation. Listening to reply is different from listening to ignite. As the thinker, knowing you will not be interrupted frees you truly to think for yourself* (p. 33).

There's a sort of magic that happens when we truly attend to one another, when we offer our undivided attention and listen. We can all learn to give and receive the benefits of attention to change our world and positively influence others. Every important meeting, conversation or sale where you want to persuade somebody to buy your idea requires a huge dose of listening. If you don't notice what's working and what isn't, if you can't pick up non-verbal clues, if you don't ask the really important questions and then sit back and listen then you're almost certain to fail. There's no greater gift we can give to others than our undivided attention and there's no more important skill we can practise if we want to increase our influence.

Leonard Waks of Temple University, Philadelphia, believes that simply listening in silence may not be sufficient and that to be truly effective listeners we need to give others our undivided inner attention also. In 2008 Waks wrote that:

> *Maintaining outer silence is not always sufficient to counter the negative impact on listening created by the restless external questioner … To counter it, listeners may need to refrain not merely from asking questions out loud, and thus distracting speakers and obscuring their meanings, but also from entertaining inner questions and other thoughts that distract themselves as listeners from the speaker's intent (and may subtly influence the speaker as well). That is, if listeners seek to grasp speakers' full intent, they will do well to maintain an inner silence.*
>
> **(Waks, L, 2008, Listening from silence: inner composure and engagement, p. 67)**

Build your skill

While hearing is easy, really listening and paying full attention is not, but if you practise a little and often, you will soon build your awareness of the differences between the two and strengthen your listening muscles.

Ask a friend or colleague to do the next exercise with you.

Exercise

Find a quiet spot where you will not be interrupted.

1. Spend five minutes listening to the other person. Feel free to let your mind wander. Allow your gaze to roam and your body to move.

2. Take a second five minutes but this time hold eye contact with the other person. (The other person's gaze will most likely wander so this should feel comfortable for both of you. Every time the other person's gaze comes back to you they will notice that you are still paying attention.)

3. Remain relaxed but as physically still as you can.

4. Every time a thought comes into your mind, gently let it go and focus on what the other person is saying.

5. Swap places and then compare the different experiences.

Listening to unlock

So how can listening help us sell our idea or persuade the other person? What is it we should be listening for when we want to influence somebody?

Values, beliefs and motivation

Listen for what the person most values, for their deeply held beliefs. If you mismatch these you are unlikely to persuade the other person. What values are most important to them? What are they motivated by? There will be many clues both in what the other person says but also the way they say it. Once you become a great listener you can really tune in to the whole conversation.

Emotions and energy

Listen in order to become aware of the emotions and energy of the other person. By matching these more closely you will create rapport and empathy. Think about how you might feel when you're angry and the person tries to 'calm you down' in a soft spoken voice. It's a bit like pouring oil on the fire. A really effective way to manage strong emotions is to deliver a positive message but at the same volume and intensity as the other person. The same goes for someone whose energy is low and they are emotionally upset – match their volume and energy first and, once you create rapport and understanding, you can slowly turn up the emotional dial and support them to move to a more positive state of mind.

Voice tone and body language

Notice the tone of voice – it's not *what* people say but *how* they say it that tells you what you most need to know. Pick up the body language signals to tune into the non-verbal conversation that's taking place between you.

The table below presents some Dos and Don'ts which will help you win influence when you need to tune in to the other person, build rapport and respond as much to what's not being said as the content.

How to lose influence when listening	How to win influence when listening
Focus solely on content. **Risk:** you miss the point. You fail to pick up all the other subtle clues the person is communicating.	Focus on voice tone and body language as well as content. **Benefit:** you are able to respond to the whole conversation, both verbal and non-verbal.
Thinking their issue is exactly the same as one you've experienced. Telling them what you did in the same situation. **Risk:** make false assumptions that close down thinking and miss finding the best solution.	Ask questions that help to clarify the issue as experienced by the other person so they can continue to do their best thinking. **Benefit:** they come up with a much better solution that works for them.
Allow the mind to wander (people can always tell when you've stopped listening). **Risk:** missing important information, breaking rapport, being rude.	Keep your mind open and focused on the other person. **Benefit:** show respect and build rapport. Pick up on important information.
Break eye contact. **Risk:** sending the message that something else is more interesting than the person you're listening to.	Maintain eye contact all the time. **Benefit:** helps you stay focused, helps the other person feel 'seen' and listened to, shows attention and respect.
Give advice. **Risk:** closing down the other person's thinking and creativity.	Allow them to find their own best solution. **Benefit:** build their confidence and ability to think creatively.
Interrupt. **Risk:** you lose the sale, you miss the solution, you undermine the relationship.	Wait until they have finished *thinking* (not talking) and notice the difference. **Benefit:** you create a sense of ease and encourage deeper thinking. You build rapport.

▶

How to lose influence when listening	How to win influence when listening
You're uncomfortable with silence so you step in as soon as the other person has stopped talking.	You're able to sit quietly with the other person and give them as much time as they need to finish their thinking.
Risk: you increase your own internal anxiety and interrupt their thinking. You break rapport.	**Benefit:** you are seen as a valued colleague, friend or leader.

What are the benefits of deep listening?

You can test this for yourself. Think about your own experience.

➡ In the presence of deep attention we feel *seen* and *heard.*

➡ Listening to someone helps them to do their absolute best thinking and come up with their own solutions.

➡ Listening shows respect, recognition and strengthens the relationship.

➡ People feel valued, important, acknowledged, which increases their commitment to the relationship, team, group or organisation.

➡ Listening builds trust.

➡ Being truly listened to fulfils one of our deepest human needs.

After doing the following exercise you will be aware of how effective a listener you are. You can now practise this exercise to take your listening to the next level:

Week One: On two days a week make a conscious commitment to talk 25 per cent less than you normally would and use that time to listen to others more deeply.

Week Two: On two days a week make a conscious effort to talk 50 per cent less than you normally would and use that time to listen more deeply.

Week Three: On two days a week make a conscious effort to talk 75 per cent less than you normally would and use that time to listen more deeply.

1. How did you do each week?

2. How do others around you respond when you talk less?

3. What emotions does this practice bring up for you?

4. How liberating does it feel to let go of talking?

Listen out and listen in

While it's important to listen to others we also need to pay attention to what's happening for us on the inside. Listening to our own internal voice, our automatic responses and our emotional reactions can help us develop our own emotional self-awareness. We need to tune in to us in order to learn. It can be really difficult to listen to others when we are over-whelmed, stressed or under a lot of pressure – build in time to notice what's going on for you.

Put aside some quiet time each day to listen to your own internal voice and to notice what's going on for you. Notice if you have any of these voices in your head:

Critical voice: Do you criticise yourself? If you do, what causes the voice to start up? What things do you say to yourself? How can you practise being kinder to yourself? How can you reduce the voice of the inner critic in your own mind?

Voice of fear and anxiety: When you are under pressure to perform do you hear a voice of anxiety and fear? What do you say to yourself? How can you better support yourself under pressure? How can you take the pressure off? Use the techniques in Chapter 1 – morning pages, mindfulness, exercise and visualisation – to support yourself if you are self-critical or anxious.

How can we encourage others to listen?

Do you know people who continually interrupt? What happens to your emotional state when people keep interrupting you? How can you influence others to listen more deeply and with better attention? There are some people who are poor listeners and quick to interrupt. If you know somebody like this, the first thing to do is notice your own reaction. Do you get angry? Do you withdraw? Do you avoid them? Or do you interrupt back and get into a conversational tennis match? If you react in any of these ways you may be reinforcing their behaviour. Here are some suggestions for dealing with people who are not good listeners:

➡ **Listen more, listen better:** If you tend to withdraw your attention from the person they will most likely sense it and unconsciously continue to talk in order 'to be heard'. The next time you speak give them your full and undivided attention and create a sense of ease for them. Take the approach that you will be the best listener first rather than internally 'stonewalling' them. When people feel really heard they are able to relax and become more prepared to listen in return.

→ **Ask for equality:** If the person continues to take the lion's share of the conversation, ask for equality. Get yourself in a positive frame of mind and think about something you would like to speak to them about. Ask them for some of their time for you to explore the topic and for them to simply listen. Make the ground rules clear: you are not looking for advice but it would help for you to think through something with them. By framing it as a favour and being clear about what your needs are this will give them an opportunity to practise listening and you the opportunity to be listened to by them. Set a time boundary, say five to ten minutes. Then swap. By doing this exercise you may well help to break the unconscious pattern. You will also create a better balance between listening and being listened to.

→ **Say it like it is:** If you tell somebody how important it is to you to be listened to equally and they continue to interrupt ask them for permission for you to point this out gently when they do this. You might be surprised at how effective this is and how valued it is by the other person. People are often aware of their own habits, but might find them difficult to change. You will be offering them a gift if you do this with compassion and then reinforce how much you appreciate them listening.

→ **Team talk:** If you are a manager you are in the best position to make deep listening a habit in your team. For a section of your team meetings, be explicit that everyone will give their opinion or views on a topic and the rest of the team will listen with real attention. Again set the ground rules: when people listen they should maintain eye contact and pay attention. Give every person equal time.

What leaders can learn about the art of listening

When I worked as the head of communications at one of the largest British insurance companies, I was asked to help the leadership team communicate the new business strategy to employees following the financial crisis. The team spent months reviewing the business and wanted to implement a new strategy. We agreed to hold a series of roadshows with employees, 70 per cent of whom worked in the call centres dealing directly with customer claims. We agreed a fairly gruelling schedule of two events a day with short lunch breaks and long journeys to cover multiple sites across the UK and Ireland. The events comprised a formal business presentation followed by small table discussions with a member of the senior leadership team facilitating.

The first day was tough. Many employees sat with their arms across their chests and said very little during the table discussion. It was not what the senior team were expecting. Over the five weeks, we held 33 events with the team facilitating hundreds of table discussions and facing many questions, challenges and criticisms. The new business strategy was all about how to improve customer service. Yet every place we went we heard the same story: employees said the business made this almost impossible.

One call centre worker called Jane stood up and told us about a phone call she'd had with an 89-year-old Welsh woman called Edith whose house had been flooded. When she took the call, Edith was knee deep in water sobbing and asked Jane to help save her possessions. Jane stayed on the phone for over half an hour talking to Edith about her family, keeping her calm while her colleague called the ambulance. The call centre Jane works in is managed by targets and goals; calls are timed, logged and evaluated on results and results have little to do with empathy. Jane didn't hit her targets that morning and received a warning from her supervisor.

Jane's story was not unusual. Other employees were angry that pensioners who had been loyal customers for years paid the highest premiums because they didn't compare deals. The team heard similar stories everywhere they went. It was no wonder they got such a cool reception from employees. The roadshows were a sobering experience: it took humility for the executive team to face the gap between their vision and the business reality, and courage for employees to speak honestly to senior executives. But these conversations started a small revolution in the business and led to a complete rethink of what needed to be done.

I've spent years in corporate businesses that say they want to listen to employees but found few who really mean it. Listening can be uncomfortable. Listening sometimes means you have to face uncomfortable truths. In some situations there's nothing quite as scary as sitting down face to face and having authentic, uncomfortable conversations – but listening to your employees might just be the most radical thing you can do to improve your business.

Great leaders are great listeners

If you're a leader of a business, a community or a team, here are four compelling reasons why listening can make the difference between success and failure.

Listen to think

When we listen to one another we raise the quality of everybody's thinking. That means that we can find better solutions to our problems and generate the most creative ideas. If you are prepared to listen, people feel safe to explore and start to tell you what they really think. People feel respected and important. Soon you begin to unearth the wisdom of everyone not just those that talk the loudest or are the most senior.

Listen to learn

If you have the courage to listen, you will learn about what's really going on in your relationship, business or team.

Listen to grow

Listening is the soil in which everything else grows: relationships, respect, trust, equality, wisdom, understanding and success.

Listen to connect

Once listening is a valued behaviour in your business you change the quality and balance of everything that is human: your people will never be the same. You won't need to spend money on expensive campaigns to improve employee engagement because you will be living it.

Who should leaders listen to?

There are many voices that will offer you wisdom, insight, knowledge and inspiration, but here are the most important ones for leaders.

Listen to those who don't agree with you. *Avoid groupthink*	Listen to the mavericks, to those who disagree with you. Listen to outsiders and critics. Avoid repeating the mistakes of the global financial experts who were blinded by groupthink and mocked the few brave souls who dared to challenge the dominant thinking.
Listen to your team. Listen more deeply. *Prepare the leaders of the future*	Make team meetings the time for robust debate and challenge. Your team will become the leaders of the future.

▶

Listen to employees. *Keep your fingers on the pulse*	Listen to those who are close to customers and who know what's really happening in the business. Institutionalise listening in your business.
Listen to customers and competitors. *Get an outside perspective*	Take a fresh look at your business from the outside and listen to your customers and competitors.

The hidden power of questions

What are some practical ways to make listening a positive habit of influence in your life and business? Simple – ask great questions then sit back and listen to the answers.

If the quality of the thinking we do can change our lives, then questions are the secret weapon in directing our thinking to the place it most needs to go. When we ask the right question of others we encourage them to dig deeper in their thinking and we signal that we want to listen more deeply. When we make statements, or give opinions we can close down the other person's thinking, but when we ask questions we move people into creative thinking mode.

Different types of questions and how they direct our attention

Questions that clarify

At the beginning of an important project, a new job, a sale or when scoping work for a new client, asking the right questions will set you up for success. Resist the temptation to jump into 'doing' and take time to understand their requirements fully. It can be difficult and costly to realise half way through a project that you've not fully clarified what the other person really wants, or that you're operating on assumptions.

Use these questions to help you clarify what somebody wants:

- ➡ What does success look like for you?
- ➡ What's your outcome?
- ➡ How will you know you have been successful? What evidence will you need?
- ➡ How can I best help you?
- ➡ What else do we need to consider?
- ➡ Who else do we need to consider?
- ➡ What have we missed?
- ➡ What is it that you don't want?
- ➡ What's your fear?
- ➡ What can go wrong?
- ➡ What's not possible and why?
- ➡ What do we need (and who do we need to include) to ensure we get our outcome?
- ➡ What would x (somebody you admire or respect) say about this issue?

Goal questions

Use these questions to clarify goals and increase motivation:

- ➡ What's your goal?
- ➡ How badly do you want it?
- ➡ If you don't do x, what will happen?
- ➡ If you knew you couldn't fail, what would you do?
- ➡ If you had all the resources you need, what would you do then?
- ➡ When you imagine yourself doing x what will it feel like (look like)?
- ➡ If you imagine yourself in x time having been successful, what advice would you give yourself now?
- ➡ If you imagine yourself in a year's time (or longer) what would you say to yourself about this issue?

Appreciative questions

Use these questions to generate appreciative thinking:

➡ What's the *best* thing about x?

➡ What is working well?

➡ What's the most recent success you've had?

➡ What do you most appreciate about x?

➡ What's one of your best qualities?

➡ What do you need to do to make this even better?

➡ What will it feel like when x has finished and you've been really successful?

➡ What resources do you already have that will help you achieve x?

➡ What have you learned that will help us be successful next time?

➡ What was the best thing about not getting x?

All these questions presuppose a positive situation, characteristic or outcome. They bring up specific memories or images and positive emotion.

Uncovering questions

Use these questions when you need to uncover:

➡ What are we avoiding?

➡ Have we clearly defined the outcome?

➡ What do we need that we don't have?

➡ What's not being said?

➡ What are we missing?

➡ What have we not noticed?

➡ What do we want instead?

➡ What's the most important issue we should be dealing with right now?

➡ Who have we not included in the conversation that needs to be included?

- ➡ Is there something else we should be doing instead of this?
- ➡ What's the most important question we need to ask?
- ➡ If we don't achieve our outcome, what is the next best thing?
- ➡ If we don't deal with this, what's the price we will have to pay?

Learning questions

Use these questions when you need to generate learning:

- ➡ What was the most important thing we learnt from x?
- ➡ How can we use the experience to improve?
- ➡ What would we do differently next time?
- ➡ How can we share what we've learnt with others?
- ➡ What do other people know that will help us?
- ➡ Where can we use this knowledge or experience again?
- ➡ What do we need to find out?
- ➡ Who is the expert that we need to learn from?
- ➡ Who does this best?
- ➡ What skill or knowledge would make the difference here?
- ➡ What surprised us the most about what we have done?

Questions to avoid

The question 'Why?' should be used with caution because it assumes somebody needs to explain or justify themselves such as 'Why did you do that?' The normal response to a 'why' question is to justify which brings out feelings of defensiveness. There are many other 'rhetorical-why' questions that are unhelpful and should be avoided, questions such as 'What's wrong with X?' or 'Why can't I ...?' These questions presuppose that there *is* something wrong or that you *can't* do something, and this is not useful if your intention is to have a conversation that generates positive feelings and outcomes. Notice where questions take people's thinking and craft them to direct attention to positive and productive outcomes. If something was not successful it's more helpful to ask 'What did we learn?' Or, 'What would have helped us get a better/different outcome?' Or, 'What do we need to do differently?'

Brain Rules:

1. We can only focus on one task at a time – listening requires our focused attention.
2. We strengthen the neural pathways for listening through practice.
3. Deep attention puts others at ease and helps them do their best thinking. Build the habit into your meetings, conversations and whenever you want to sell or convince somebody.

Top Tips:

1. Listen to the whole conversation: voice tone, body language, what's not being said.
2. Listen with deep curiosity and non-judgement.
3. Be comfortable with silence.
4. Practise a little every day until listening with true attention becomes a habit.

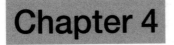

Chapter 4

Words change minds: the language of influence

Our language influences our perceptions.

Peter Senge, Leadership in living organisations, p. 75.

The building blocks of language

Learning is for babies. We are born with the ability to hear and to make every sound in every language in the world (which is around 6800 languages). Every language is complex and includes subtle distinctions which even native speakers may not be aware of, yet by the age of five or six years children across the world become fluent in their native tongue.

In terms of neuroscience, we are born with the mental *scaffolding* already in place to learn language. Language is made up of sounds (words) that prompt our brain to convert the word into a meaningful representation.

The power of language to direct attention

Language can unconsciously affect the decisions we make in everyday life. The social psychologist, John Bargh, from Yale University, has spent years researching the unconscious causes of our attitudes and motivations to find out how much of our social behaviour is affected by subliminal stimuli such as the words we see in advertising, or words we pick up in conversations on how this impacts on our decisions. Scientists call this 'priming'.

Case study

In one experiment, some subjects were asked to read words which could be unconsciously related to the elderly, for example, *bingo*. When these subjects left the laboratory, they walked more slowly compared to those who had not read the words. In another experiment, those who were given words related to *achievement* performed better in a demanding word search than those who had not. It's not only language that primes our unconscious responses; when the scientists put a backpack in the room it prompted more cooperative behaviour from the group whereas a briefcase prompted more competitive behaviour.

There's a significant body of research into the effects of priming on consumers by the use of both symbols and language and much of the research challenges the idea that we are consciously making many of our choices. Bargh argues that much of the mental processing that drives our decision-making takes place outside of our ▶

conscious awareness and that priming means many of our choices are made as if we are on auto-pilot. Bargh says of free will:

> *Clearly it is motivating for each of us to believe we are better than average, that bad things happen to other people, not ourselves, and that we have free-agentic control over our own judgments and behavior—just as it is comforting to believe in a benevolent God and justice for all in an afterlife. But the benefits of believing in free will are irrelevant to the actual existence of free will. A positive illusion, no matter how functional and comforting, is still an illusion.*

Sources: Bargh, J A *et al*. (1996) The automaticity of social behavior: direct effects of trait concept and stereotype activation on action.
Bargh, J A *et al*. (2001) The automated will: nonconscious activation and pursuit of behavioral goals.

How neuroscience explains why the message you send is not the message received

If our brains are organised to understand and communicate with others from the day we are born, why do we sometimes get it so wrong? How is it that, even when we speak the same language, we can feel as if we don't? How does language get to be so tricky? And how can we make sure we use it as a powerful tool for influence? Let's start by looking at how our brain processes a single 'packet' of language such as the simple noun 'cat'. Put this book down for a moment. Close your eyes and think of a cat. What image came into your mind? How long did it take you? Did you notice the sequence your brain went through to make your choice? Probably not; the neurological activity that takes place to process language happens so quickly and involves a process that goes something like this – first, the brain has to recognise a group of letters as a 'word' that belongs to the language rules coded into your mind. If you were asked to think of a 'dvpt', your brain instinctively knows not to bother starting a search because the sequence of letters breaks the unconscious rules of English. But once your brain recognises that a group of letters (or a spoken word) is a 'word' it performs what linguists call a 'trans derivational search' and scans *across* billions of smaller bits of information stored in different areas of the brain.

However, given that we are likely to have many experiences of cats, how do we go about selecting one particular cat above all others? Everything we experience is coded into the brain with an 'affective tag' – whether it is associated with pain or pleasure. So the first rule of recall is to search for the strongest emotional associations with a word which could be negative or positive (a much loved cat, or a cat that terrified us). Emotional memories are stored deep in the limbic system so this is the first place the brain searches, triggering associated sensory memories which may in turn generate images in the visual cortex, tactile associations in the sensory cortex and auditory associations in the auditory cortex.

When the memory of your 'cat' pops into your mind, it does so as an instantaneous, coherent single memory; but your brain has just performed the hugely complex task of reassembling an experience stored in parcelled *bits* of information across the various brain cortices at warp speed. If you ask ten people in a room to think of a cat, no two cats will be the same. Cat owners or those who strongly dislike cats come up with a memory first because their brains hold strong emotional associations with the word. But those who have no strong emotional associations take the longest time to choose, for them all cats are pretty much the same: Garfield, the neighbour's cat, the cat next door. Yet everyone selects on the basis of their personal experience and everyone's cat will pop into their mind with their own visual, auditory, kinaesthetic and emotional associations.

The resulting emotional tag increases the likelihood of the recall of the event/object. This is all about the emotional flavour of the memory and the associations that are triggered. Figure 4.1 gives examples of positive and negative emotional tags associated with the word 'cat'.

If the word 'cat' has so many different associations, think about the variety of personal associations with more loaded words, such as God, family, school, friends, work, money, sex and love. These are not only likely to differ between individuals but also within each person. How has the meaning of these words above changed from when you were six years old compared to now?

Exercise

Take one of the words above or any word you choose. Sit quietly for a moment and close your eyes. Say the word to yourself and, as you do so, pay close attention to any images, feelings, other thoughts and words and memories that come into your mind. Pause.

Resist the temptation to carry on thinking about what you've experienced in the mind and keep watching what arises. Repeat the word again and see what arises.

Try it with a friend and see what you notice.

We think of language as universal and shared and of words as 'fixed' descriptors of a simple truth; what could be more straightforward than a simple noun such as 'cat'? How can we each have such different emotional responses, internal images

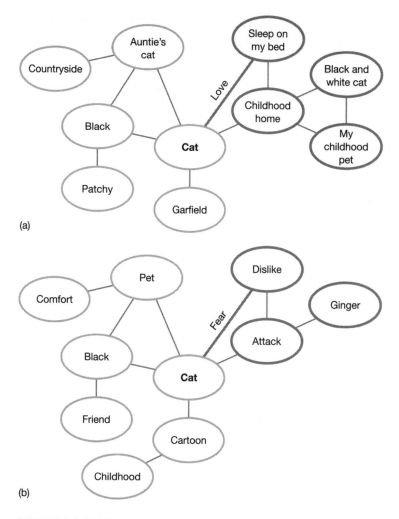

FIGURE 4.1 (a) While your brain may generate a number of memories of cats, the one that will come to the forefront is the one with the strongest emotional tag. (b) If you were attacked by a cat as a child, the emotional tag for this semantic node will be strong but also negative so you will very quickly remember that cat and possibly experience sensations of fear in the body.

and meanings? Words are powerful containers of personal meaning and sometimes the message you think you're sending is not necessarily the message received.

> **1st rule of language as a tool of influence:**
>
> Remember that *my cat is not your cat* – once we understand more about how our minds process language we can use language that directs the mind of the other person to where we actually want it to go.

Let people make connections

So once we've learnt simple words as children – a single word for a single object – we take the next step on the linguistic ladder and begin to group words into what's known as *classifications*. We now start to move into more abstract use of language. For instance, think of the word 'fruit'; there's no such thing as *fruit* there are only individual items of fruit – a banana, an apple, an orange – that our mind groups together to understand the concept *fruit*.

We're not conscious of what our brain is doing to process the word *fruit* because it's working at a speed which (even our own brain) finds hard to contemplate – 20 billion calculations per second. And then our brain does something even more elegant; it understands *fruit* by connecting the word inside a web of semantic meaning (see Fig. 4.2): ideas of eating, nourishment, shopping or gathering, peeling, colour, texture, smell, memories. Semantic meaning is different if you live in Asia or Europe because you will group different individual fruits together, but each person will have different types of fruit. A child might 'hate' the idea of eating 'fruit' while someone who is health conscious might 'love' the idea. So while the word will have its own emotional 'tag' for each person, the

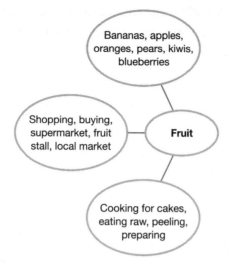

FIGURE 4.2 We understand language through a rich network of unconscious semantic meaning.

brain is working at a more complex level to understand what the word means. But it's still relatively easy for our brain to *unpack* a classification such as fruit because what's inside the classification are individual sensory-specific items that we have experience of: bananas, apples, oranges.

But when we start to use abstract language (which for anyone who works in business is words like *strategic advantage*), the brain goes off to search for feelings, colour, texture, images and comes back empty-handed. So by using these sorts of abstract words you are asking the brain to climb right to the top of the linguistic ladder and then to engage in the most *brain hungry* processing possible.

Jargon is hard work for the brain

Jargon is one of the biggest offenders when it comes to influential language because it's abstract, conceptual language that is harder for the brain to understand and create internal associations with. We know that emotions are the sparks that motivate us to do things (or avoid things) and that energise us when we're listening to other people. When a speaker uses too much jargon, or doesn't give the audience quick ways to understand and interpret it, it simply switches off the brains of the audience. If a CEO said in a presentation that the business plans to *leverage its advantaged assets* your brain tries to unpack what individual items might belong inside the classification – it could be your products, or services, or new customers or a whole other range of things, but whatever you come up with you will be making a guess. So when you ask your audience to guess at the meaning of your communication you are failing to influence.

When we use simple sensory-specific language, the network easily spreads outwards. This doesn't take a lot of effort for the brain because much of it is drawn up automatically and we add and embellish ourselves. All the content is personally meaningful (which the brain loves). In contrast, when we work with high-level abstract concepts and jargon, the process starts several layers out and we ask the brain to work back to find the specifics of the classification. These processes are illustrated in Figure 4.3. This process of working backwards takes a lot of effort for the brain. It does not flow easily, is not personally relevant and is difficult to understand. A spreading network is less effort for the brain than a contracting network. You can think about these two brain processes as water flowing effortlessly outwards, or like trying to push water uphill.

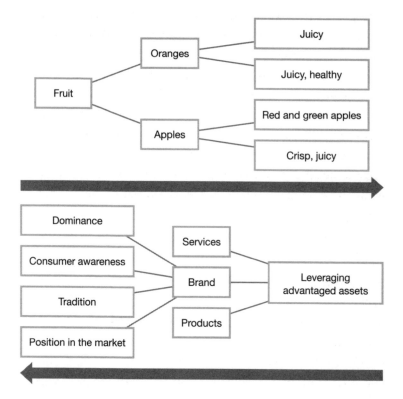

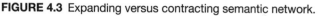

FIGURE 4.3 Expanding versus contracting semantic network.

2nd rule of language as a tool of influence:

It's easier for networks in the brain to expand than to contract. The brain has a propensity for mental proliferation – semantic networks are the building blocks of this.

Jargon creates barriers

There are other problems with jargon that make it toxic when you want to communicate your message because jargon communicates whether you're an insider or an outsider in a group. Have you ever started a new job and spent the first month trying to get to grips with the acronyms, sayings, terminology and jargon of the organisation? When I joined a large global bank, I remember the anxiety I felt when confronted with a new language. A year later I could use many new words in conversation but, as a communicator, when I sat down and tried to decode them for employees to make the communication more concrete and simple I struggled because my mind couldn't create an internal representation of words like risk weighted assets, capital adequacy ratio, EPS, ROCE; they floated around in my mind – vague and colourless. Of course jargon plays an important role (as a short cut for a wealth of complex ideas and concepts) for senior bankers, financial analysts and specialists, but the problem comes when it's overused and dominates the conversation in the business. Because jargon communicates a subtle and implicit question (are you one of us?), it creates *insiders and outsiders*. Business jargon is used by leaders and middle managers (and rarely by people on the shopfloor) so it reinforces an *'us and them'* mentality and, if we're not careful, we can create a linguistic class system that keeps people in different tribes.

Because CEOs spend years developing their understanding of the business and technical terminology they feel very connected to it, but the average employee has not developed their own rich associations; they are just learning by rote.

3rd rule of language as a tool of influence:

Avoid using jargon and abstract language if you want to connect with your audience and include everyone in the conversation.

If you are a specialist, such as a CEO, a scientist or a technology wizard, you will stand out from the crowd, educate and inspire your audience when you are able to share your specialist knowledge in a way that is easy to understand and to remember. There's nothing quite as inspiring as finding out about new ideas in fields that are unfamiliar to you, and those who are able to bridge the communication gap between their speciality and the rest of us are truly great communicators. Chances are they will have found a way to turn the techno-babble into pictures, emotions and colour by using stories, metaphors, similes and images to help your brain make a connection between something you already know and something that is new. That's where metaphors and storytelling (Chapter 5) can help you build a linguistic bridge with your audience.

Tips for keeping your message simple:

1. Be aware that jargon has to be learnt and then reverse-coded/decoded every time it's used – this is effortful for the brain.

2. Converting complex information into easily digestible and tasty nuggets flavoured with emotion and colour will make it memorable.

What we need to stop saying

Negative language creates negative feelings

Using negative language directs someone's attention *away from* what we want. Imagine you're in an exercise class working really hard, with perspiration dripping down your face, your t-shirt is stuck to your back, you're gasping for breath and on the edge of your physical limit when the personal trainer shouts in a loud voice, *'Don't stop!'* Your brain finds mental associations with the word 'stop', such as *slowing down, breathing normally, relaxing your muscles* and then has to reverse these images to understand the instruction is actually to *'keep going'*. If you say to a child 'don't fall' or 'don't touch' you're directing their attention to create an internal mental picture of *falling* or *touching* something in order for them to understand your instruction. Yet we use this language all the time.

Case study

When I worked in communications in a large global bank we were asked to put together a campaign that would help to change the behaviour of employees and make them more security conscious when handling customer data. The campaign was a response to the bank being fined £5m by the FSA (Financial Services Authority) following a string of IT security failures, and the senior IT director suggested we communicate the '10 things not to do'. But by understanding that the brain processes negative instructions by creating mental images associated with the things we *don't* want, we developed a campaign using positive messages; instead of saying 'Don't leave your laptop unlocked' we used a series of questions, such as 'Safe to leave?', 'Safe to send?', to prompt people to think consciously about their actions and to allow them to make an informed decision. Messages that string a list of 'do not' instructions together also create internal triggers (internal images, memories and feelings) of being a child at school or at home when we were 'in trouble' so they can be counter-productive when you want to build understanding and rapport with your audience.

Our brains are also not designed to remember a list of 10 things. There's a rule of memory which says that, on average, we can remember 'seven, plus or minus two'; what this means is that most people can remember seven things, some people can only remember five, and others can remember up to nine. So as a communicator it's wise to limit your list to seven (and shorten it if at all possible). If you think about how the brain recalls telephone numbers (normally 11 digits), we group them into smaller chunks of three or four digits which are much easier to remember. If you really want people to remember some important points or instructions, avoid creating automatic lists of 'the top 10'.

We launched our campaign at the bank with seven important messages for employees (we had to wean the IT Director off the 10 commandments syndrome), but it would have been more memorable to stick to five items. Once you understand these simple rules of language and how your brain processes your messages you can make sure your messages stick.

Tips for influential language:

1. Tell people what you want them to do (use positive language).

2. Adding 'don't' to an instruction forces the brain to do an extra level of cognitive processing.

3. If you want people to recall information keep your lists to between five and seven main points.

Turning verbs into nouns (nominalisation)

Proper nouns describe things in our world – a tree, a river, a boat – but there's another type of noun we often use called a nominalisation; the words 'relationship' and 'communication' are all instances of nominalisations. Let's unpack the word relationship; there is no such thing as a relationship – a relationship exists only in language and not in our lived experience. In our real life, relationships are the sum total of a whole lot of things we *do* when we are relating to other people; talking, sharing, listening, etc. But when we turn all of these activities (verbs) into a single noun, we end up *fixing it* in our mind.

For example, imagine that your best friend comes up and says to you: 'My relationship has failed.' How do you immediately feel? What's the first image that comes into your mind? It feels a bit like a *concrete* statement of fact (concrete is a good way to remember how nominalisations work in the mind because they 'fix' something). But part of the problem with the statement is the word itself (*relationship*) because our thinking is directed away from all of the different parts of relating to others. As soon as we turn (dead) language back into (living) experience, we open up new possibilities and new ways of thinking. We can do this quite easily by putting the suffix – *ing* – back onto many words.

Let's take a look at how this works. You could ask your friend: 'What specifically is it that's not working in the way you are <u>relating</u> to X?' Their attention now has to turn inside so they can begin to search for things to help them answer your question; what is it that is specifically happening? Where is it happening? When is it happening? Who is doing the action? They have to move back into the world of lived experiences.

Moreover, by including in the question the words 'you are relating', we introduce the idea of *agency* (a term used to describe the capacity we have to *act* in the world), so the person begins to focus on what it is they may like to *do* about the situation. It invites action or consideration of action. This also avoids making the assumption that the 'other person' is to blame for what's not working and draws the person's attention to their own sense of agency so they can consider new possibilities, options, choices and actions.

Another example of a nominalisation is the word *confidence.* This does not exist; you cannot go into a shop and buy it (it's not a book). Confidence is made up of many different skills, behaviours and beliefs. The skills involved in *confidenting* (grammatically incorrect but a more useful way to think about the activity) can be practised so that we *become* more confident and continue to become more confident the more we practise. Nominalising verbs can be a powerful linguistic trap – because it can stop us from seeing what's really happening.

Remember that language is all about *directing our attention* and nominalisations can stop our attention from going to the places we need to go. *How we think* about something makes all the difference in the world; the ability to think clearly, question wisely and use our mind to help us overcome problems and find new solutions is the most powerful gift of influential communication. If you are a coach, parent, friend or colleague, use this very simple language rule to help others get 'unstuck'. And this rule applies to your own internal self-talk so try out the exercise below and notice the difference denominalising your life can make.

Exercise

Turn the following words into verbs:

Credibility
Persuasion
Communication
Influence

4th rule of language as a tool of influence:

Turn dead language back to living experiences. Activate your brain by activating your language – this encourages more 'movement' in the mind and in finding more creative solutions.

Shifty language

Nominalisations are sometimes used by businesses and politicians to shift responsibility for a particular decision or action – for example, if a CEO presents a decision as being made by the *leadership* of the business (rather than himself or the leaders in the executive team). There's no such thing as leadership, only people who lead and who are responsible for taking decisions. The word *management* is also often used in this context.

These words are often used when leaders want to distance themselves from 'blame' or responsibility, but the danger for leaders who use these when delivering difficult messages is that they distance themselves from employees and lose trust and credibility.

Another example of shifty language is the phrase 'It has been decided' which only begs the question 'By whom?' One of the most infamous examples of this use of language was when Donald Rumsfeld, the US Secretary of State in George Bush's administration, said, when responding to journalists about the Haditha massacre (where 24 unarmed Iraqi men, women and children were killed by a group of United States Marines), that: 'Things that shouldn't happen do happen in war.' Or, in street slang, 'Shit happens. Get over it.'

The author Henry Hitchings decribed this phenomenon very clearly:

> *Nominalizations give priority to actions rather than to the people responsible for them. Sometimes this is apt, perhaps because we don't know who is responsible or because responsibility isn't relevant. But often they conceal power relationships and reduce our sense of what's truly involved in a transaction. As such, they are an instrument of manipulation, in politics and in business. They emphasize products and results, rather than the processes by which products and results are achieved.*
>
> **(Hitchings, H, 2013, The dark side of verbs-as-nouns)**

5th rule of language as a tool of influence:

When we want to influence others to support us, we need to use open and honest communication and acknowledge who is taking decisions.

What we need to start saying

Metaphors

Metaphorical language turns complex information into a brain-friendly format so we can *map over* knowledge from something we have prior experience of to something that is new or different. When we hear metaphorical stories, our brain searches for similar experiences and we activate a part called the insula, which helps us relate emotionally to the story. An example of using metaphor to create a bridge between shared experience and something new and unknown is when we use the metaphor of the brain as a computer: this triggers many other associations and images such as *coding, being hardwired, connected,* the brain as a *processor* of information, or holding information in *bits*. Because we already hold sensory-specific images in our mind about computers (boxes, wires, information flows, screens, electricity, programmes), it's easy for our mind to use these hooks to create internal representations of how the brain works.

But while metaphors are often useful shortcuts, *the brain as computer* metaphor also constricts and limits our understanding – perhaps the brain is not so much a discrete piece of wetware (another metaphor) but a more complex, connected, organic and embedded process? By mapping an organic process to a physical, electrical, man-made object, we may also constrain understanding, so choose your metaphors wisely; think about the internal representations and feelings you want to evoke in your audience when you use a particular metaphor.

Understanding metaphor takes quite a lot of brain effort and requires that we use both left and right regions of the inferior frontal gyrus (to understand the concept), the superior temporal gyrus on the right side (to understand the context) and, finally, the anterior cingulate that helps us to focus long enough to work through the metaphor (see Fig. 4.4). But while it takes effort for the brain, it's also very satisfying because it gives us a broad and rich semantic network that allows us to cross-reference and build a rich image and deeper understanding. Once you have a metaphor that works for you it helps to build layer upon layer of meaning. If we hold a metaphor of the brain like a computer in mind then each time we learn about a new part of the brain, or another way that it processes, we continue to build up metaphoric connections which help us understand and remember.

Metaphors can also help get our message across with the least possible resistance in the minds of the audience. People don't question metaphors in the way that they question data, facts, statistics and other information. When we're presented with facts our minds are more likely to question and ask 'Is it credible?', 'What's the evidence?', 'Who said so?' etc. We use different parts of our brain when we are faced with facts (the more discerning areas that look for validation) than metaphors (the more visual and emotional parts of the brain).

Think about what comes to mind when faced with the metaphor of the 'American Dream', as opposed to a US politician delivering the dry details of a specific policy. If you've seen President Obama speaking at one of the big US political conventions or

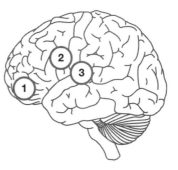

1. Inferior frontal gyrus
2. Anterior cingulate
3. Superior temporal gyrus

FIGURE 4.4 The brain regions involved in processing metaphor.

at the Presidential Inauguration, you will recall that the language used is full of metaphor, images, analogies, stories and never about dry specific policy details. Political language is the language of emotional persuasion; you might even think about it as the language of *trance* as the audience is carried along on an unquestioning emotional journey (because our brain doesn't question emotions, only 'facts'). It's not surprising that people in groups who listen to skilled communicators using metaphorical language end up being almost of 'the same mind'. Politicians and businesses are only too aware of the power of language to convince, persuade or dissuade consumers and voters.

The power of frames

Another influential language tool which is a close cousin to the metaphor is 'framing', a language tool used by influential communicators to sell and persuade. A few years ago I visited the Tate Modern art gallery on London's South Bank with a friend and asked her what she liked about a particular painting we were both looking at. She said that she loved the frame and that whenever she looked at a painting it was the frame that she noticed first. She said that the right frame could make an ordinary picture great and the wrong frame make a great picture ordinary. I was completely taken by surprise. I realised that she noticed something that I paid little or no conscious attention to at all. There are also linguistic frames that operate in exactly this way; they are outside of our conscious awareness but they have a profound effect on the way we construct meaning and interpret language. While linguistic frames are everywhere, we rarely notice them because our attention is drawn (and held) *inside* the frame.

One example of a linguistic frame is that used by the Bush administration in 2003 to introduce a new piece of legislation it called 'The Healthy Forest Restoration Act'. The Republican Party is very conscious in its use of language and has invested significant time and money in think tanks that come up with compelling linguistic frames to direct the public debate. The stated purpose of the new legislation was to reduce the risk of wild fires by thinning dense undergrowth in forested areas, but it did not come without controversy (hence the importance of the frame), and environmental groups argued that it was an environmental disaster and allowed the timber industry to make a windfall because it allowed them to cut down valuable timber previously protected by law.

By naming the legislation *The Healthy Forest Restoration Act*, the administration sought to create positive subliminal emotions in the minds of the voters. In the same way that the word *fruit* activates a rich semantic network of internal representations, *The Healthy Forest Restoration Act* activates unconscious positive feelings and associations in the minds of voters every time it is used in the press or TV. This frame is designed to create associations with *wellness, vibrancy, energy, life* **(healthy)** *and bringing something back to life, improving, regenerating (**restoration**).* By consciously using this linguistic frame, the administration sought to contain thinking (inside the frame) and close down debate. But environmental groups have become aware of the power of language in public debate and came up with their own frame to draw attention in a different direction entirely by calling the Act 'The No Tree Left Behind Act.' This frame creates very different internal associations: *destruction, desecration* and the *end of the world.*

The cognitive linguist, George Lakoff, has spent years studying the way political parties use linguistic frames to control and direct the public debate and believes that frames are so powerful that they 'trump facts'. Lakoff says,'*Every word is defined with respect to frames. You're framing all the time.*' Morality and emotion are already embedded in the way people think and the way people perceive certain words – and most of this processing happens unconsciously. (Explain yourself: George Lakoff, cognitive linguist, http://explainer.net/2011/01/george-lakoff/).

What's your frame?

Another recent example of powerful framing was when a UK lobbying group that was fighting the introduction of plain packaging on cigarette packets on behalf of a group of tobacco companies put out a press release stating that the introduction of plain packaging would *'create the perfect storm for black market expansion'*. The mental associations in this frame are of *disaster* and *criminality*. The words *'the perfect storm'* unconsciously trigger images and emotions from the Hollywood blockbuster *The Perfect Storm*; ordinary, likeable small-town fishermen being overwhelmed by a monstrous and unnatural ocean. The frame seeks to position the tobacco companies as *protectors* and *concerned corporate citizens* (why else spend money warning the public of the danger of plain packaging?). And the frame seeks to move attention (in the minds of readers) away from notions that plain, unbranded cigarette packets could potentially *'save lives'*, *'prevent further deaths from smoking-related diseases'* or even *'reduce the profits of tobacco companies'*.

Here are some other common linguistic frames used to shift opinion, focus attention and persuade people to a cause. Try them out for yourself and see what internal associations you come up with in your mind. Think about when you last saw these frames used in the press. Are you conscious of when frames are being used? By being more conscious of framing you can both question its veracity and also use framing in your own messages to direct attention and persuade people to your cause.

Tax planning as opposed to tax dodging

Companies use the term *'planning'* which is a *responsibility* frame; when we think of the word planning we think of efficiency and responsibility. In contrast the protest group UK Uncut frames the issue in terms of *'dodging'* – a moral frame because people who *dodge* are avoiding doing something that they are responsible for. *Dodgers* make other people carry their share of the work (tax) of the group and place *unfair* burdens on (poorer) citizens.

'Big Tobacco' or 'Big Pharma' as opposed to 'the tobacco industry' or 'the pharmaceutical industry'

Big implies global, multinational, conglomerates that *span country borders* and are therefore not accountable at a single country level, as opposed to *industry* which is a frame of *economic and social productivity* within the borders of a single country.

Anti-ageing as opposed to, say, moisturiser

This is an emotionally-driven *'away* from' frame that has a significant impact on consumer decision-making to buy products or services. Attention is drawn to associations with *disease, the end of life, dying*. While the word 'anti' operates in the same way as the word 'don't' we first have to think about ageing and then 'reverse' it to understand what's being said. If a product was sold by using positive language it would be called 'youth' or 'young' (some products are indeed called things like 'youth serum' but the bigger share of the market is framed in 'away from' language because fear is the most powerful motivating force there is).

The right to life as opposed to the right to choose

Both frames talk about 'rights' (inalienable, applied to everyone equally). For anti-abortionists the most basic human *right* is to life which this frame positions as a higher value than 'choice'. In this frame, attention is directed to the existence of the foetus (and not the woman). A *life* is being denied by the woman who seeks to have an abortion. For pro-abortionists, the *rights* they are seeking to protect are those of the woman – the right to choose what happens to her own body. In this frame, attention is directed to the woman (and not the foetus). Both are moral frames. A secondary frame that is used in this debate is the use of the word 'foetus' as opposed to 'unborn child'.

Frames are also values

All of the frames above are also deeply value-laden; they are not neutral and they attempt to influence our values by touching on powerful emotional triggers. Frames can be used as a negative or positive tool of influence (depending on your intention) so be aware of their power and use them wisely.

Many companies 'brand' change programmes to make them memorable. But beware of the power of the frame. If a company calls a change programme 'Together for a Better Future' and employees experience insecurity, job losses or changes to their pay and benefits, the name of the programme can become a lightning rod for dissent and anger. Think of the power of a political frame turned against the politician who uses it to influence voters as was the case when Prime Minister David Cameron said: 'We're all in this together'. Voters did not fail to notice the discrepancy between stories of bankers' bonuses, company tax havens and company tax avoidance with the idea that austerity is a shared economic reality.

Source: Gary Barker Illustration

Choose your frame wisely or it may come back to haunt you.

Exercise

1. Notice how frames are used in the press, in advertising, in politics and in public debate.

2. Next time you go shopping notice the frames that convince you to buy.

3. What frames are most commonly used in public debate and politics?

4. What values are being expressed within the frame?

5. What emotions does the frame evoke? Is it an away from or toward frame?

Presuppositions

A presupposition is 'an implicit assumption about the world or background belief relating to an utterance whose truth is taken for granted' (Wikipedia.org). When you use presuppositions you are making an assumption that something has already happened. An example of an effective presupposition was used by one of the judges on the UK TV show *The Voice* (where successful singing contestants get to choose the judge they want to be their coach) when one of the judges said to a contestant: 'I look forward to working with you and to writing songs, recording, putting out records.' The judge was using a presupposition as a way to make the contestant *imagine* these things happening in their mind. It's a very seductive technique, and one which is used subliminally to influence choice and action.

You can use presuppositions by saying things like:

➡ 'When we are all together this time next year, we will be able to look back on our successful project.' (You are presupposing that you will in fact be together at the same time in a year and that the project will be successful.)

➡ 'At our next coaching session we can review your progress.' (You are presupposing the person will book another coaching session and will have made progress.)

➡ 'I look forward to meeting up again, once you've had a chance to review the proposal.' (You are presupposing the client wants to meet again and that they will have read the proposal and be prepared to review it.)

These presuppositions are influential because they create an *imagined future* in the mind and act as subliminal command. A presupposition can persuade someone to make a choice they may not have made otherwise; how would you respond if the coach (in the second example above) said at the end of your first session: 'Think about whether you'd like to book another session and then give me a call.' The presupposition is that you need to consider whether or not you want another session (so your attention is drawn to having to make a conscious choice between two different options). This is an example of a negative frame for selling. So be conscious of your own presuppositions. The imaginary coach in the example above may have strong values about 'not being pushy' but, without realising it, they may actually be dissuading potential clients from using their services.

Use presuppositions to positively influence others at home or at work, e.g. if a colleague is having a difficult time you might say: 'Just imagine in a couple of weeks when this is all over and you've succeeded in achieving your goal.' This will help them imagine how they will feel when the pressure is off and the goal has been achieved and will help to keep them motivated.

Exercise

1. Practise using presuppositions in your work to help colleagues or your team achieve stretching goals.

2. Next time a friend is in need of encouragement, consciously use a presupposition to support them.

3. To improve your sales, use presuppositions in your website copy, promotional brochure or in meetings with clients to increase their motivation to buy your products.

Small words that have a big impact

➡ **Try:** *Try* is a linguistic get-out clause; what it really means is that we are unlikely to do something. It communicates ambivalence and uncertainty and is best avoided. Being influential and persuasive is about being honest and direct and building your credibility with others. If you're not sure whether you can do something, frame it in a positive way, e.g. 'Let me get back to you to let you know if that's possible in the timeframe.' This gives you time to work out whether it is possible and, if not, to prepare your next response.

➡ **But:** *But* tends to negate what comes before the word, e.g. 'I really like your ideas *but* …' The other person will focus on what you say after, and will interpret the first part of the sentence as little more than a way to 'soften the blow'. The word 'but' communicates your discomfort in delivering a clear message and has the effect of making your message even more negative (because why else would you need to 'soften it').

➡ **And:** Replace the word 'but' with the word 'and' when you want to communicate a difficult message: 'I really liked your ideas *and* I'd appreciate some additional information to help me decide.' This will help the person to hear *both* messages as equally important rather than the word *but* which is a *qualifier*.

➡ **Might, May:** These words are called *modal operators of possibility* (modal because they create a certain mood in the mind of the listener and *possibility* because they allow for different possible outcomes), e.g. 'You *might* like to...', or 'You *may* find this important'. You avoid presupposing something and 'soften' a suggestion. Used in the right context, they are powerful because they show respect for the other person's choice and build empathy.

➡ **Should, Must, Mustn't:** These words often evoke a negative response and are likely to make somebody think 'Says who?' or 'Why should I?' They assume that we know best, or that our opinion is the 'right' one. These are command words and to be avoided if you want to build understanding and positive influence.

Brain Rules:

1. Notice how language directs attention.
2. Use these language techniques to positively influence others.
3. Words with strong emotional tags elicit the mental representation faster and stronger (e.g. the cat example).
4. Our brain understands words in the context of a rich semantic network (e.g. fruit).
5. Use frames to direct the listener's route through their semantic network.

Top Tips:

1. Use clear, plain language to communicate your message and avoid jargon.
2. Use metaphors if you need to use abstract language to help people understand.
3. Emotion – it's your friend. It's in the room. It's everywhere. Acknowledge emotion and weave it into your message to persuade and convince.

Chapter 5

Why stories change
the world

Australian Aborigines say that the big stories – the stories worth telling and retelling, the ones in which you may find the meaning of your life – are forever stalking the right teller, sniffing and tracking like predators hunting their prey in the bush.

Robert Moss, *Dreamgates,* **p. 160.**

Outline

This chapter will show you how to use stories to persuade, motivate and sell your ideas.

1. Why we're wired for stories
2. Fact and fiction: how the brain responds
3. The science of persuasion
4. Stories simplify complexity
5. Managing change
6. Emotions sell – everything
7. Emotions drive decisions
8. Your story in a nutshell

Why we're wired for stories

Across every culture in every part of the world humans have told stories to understand, share and recall knowledge. While our ancestors sat around the camp fire listening to the tribal storyteller, we sit in cinemas, theatres or in front of TVs, computers and mobile phones to share the stories of our lives – it seems that the universal nature of storytelling explains our shared, evolved human psyche. One of the brain's unique design features is its ability to recognise patterns so that we can quickly predict what is most likely to happen next. Over the centuries, we have used narrative story structure as the most elegant way to communicate our message, our passion, our vision and who we are.

Narrative is an instantly recognisable form. When we begin to listen to a story, we know straight away that we are in familiar territory. We can sit back and relax because we know where we're going, but we also know each story offers us something new and different because no two stories are exactly the same. Why else do we have such an appetite for sequels, our favourite writers, genres, formats and styles? Our brain loves both patterns and difference. Difference means that things stand out from the crowd and similarity is familiar and comforting. When you use storytelling as part of your toolkit of influence you guarantee to make people feel both relaxed and curious – a great combination to maintain concentration and increase your ability to persuade and inspire.

Our appetite for storytelling is voracious; since the invention of the Gutenberg printing press in around 1440 humans have written around 129 864 880 books (http://www.pcworld.com/article/202803/google_129_million_different_books_have_been_published.htm) and while each book is unique we can group them into common themes. Christopher Booker, in his 2004 book *The Seven Basic Plots*, suggests that there are seven 'core' plots that comprise the most commonly recognisable narrative structures. Booker's research touches on an important idea: that when we get to the heart of the stories we tell, we notice that they share common themes: a journey taken and return; overcoming challenges; making our way in the world; a quest; comedy; tragedy and rebirth. The struggles, losses, joys and the journeys we take in our own lives are reflected back to us in the imaginary world of storytelling. Narrative structure is the most elegant form that has been honed over thousands of years to help us learn, remember and change.

But if stories are such a great way to spread ideas, to gain understanding and to motivate us, why are so many businesses so bad at telling great stories? As consumers, why are we so often confronted with dense information rather than simple explanations that help us choose and decide? And what can we learn about the art of storytelling that will help us stand out from the crowd when we want to get our ideas noticed? Let's take a look at two familiar story structures and what our brain needs to do to process the language.

Story One: The Orchestra of Recycled Parts

They race towards a rubbish truck as it empties its load at a vast landfill on the edge of the city, hauling away bin liners that overflow with household waste. Their hands are black with dirt and their faces are hidden by headscarves that protect them from the high sun.

An estimated 500 *gancheros* (recyclers) work at Catuera on the outskirts of Ascuncion, where 1.5 tonnes of rubbish are deposited daily, separating plastic and aluminium that they sell on for as little as 15p a bag.

Among the mounds of refuse, however, are used oven trays and paint pots. Cast aside by the 2 million residents of the capital of

Paraguay, they are nonetheless highly valued by Nicholas Goméz, who picks them out to make violins, guitars and cellos.

Goméz, 48, was a carpenter and *ganchero* but now works for Favio Chavez, the conductor of Paraguay's one and only land-fill orchestra. The Catuera Orchestra of Recycled Instruments is made up of 30 school-children – the sons and daughters of recyclers – whose instruments are forged from the city's rubbish. And while its members learned to play amid the flies and stench of Catuera, they are now receiving worldwide acclaim, culminating earlier this month with a concert in Amsterdam that included Pachelbel's Canon.

The project was born in 2006 when Chávez, 37, began work at the landfill as a technician, helping recyclers to classify refuse. ...

'A violin is worth more than a recycler's house,' says Chávez. 'We couldn't give a child a formal instrument as it would have put him in a difficult position. The family may have looked to sell or trade it. So we experimented with making them from the rubbish....

[Chávez] believes the mentality required to learn an instrument can be applied more widely to lift his pupils out of poverty....

Ada and Noelia Rios started attending Chávez's classes in a chapel two years ago after their grandmother signed them up. They enjoyed Chávez's strict regime, practising two hours a day at their home – and travelled around Latin America with the orchestra....

'I don't care that my violin is made out of recycled parts,' Ada says. 'To me, it's a treasure.'

Source: Gilbert, J, Paraguayan landfill orchestra makes sweet music from rub-bish, *The Guardian*, 26 April 2013 (http://www.theguardian.com/world/2013/apr/26/paraguayan-landfill-orchestra-music?CMP=twt_gu).

Story Two: Market Expansion

Further to the recent announcement about our operations in Asia and the emerging markets, today we are announcing the restructure of the technology division in order to improve our operating activities and to spearhead the identification and deployment of initiatives that will serve to increase the strategic capacity and viability of our newly-acquired European business. Now, more than ever, we need to deliver an improved multidisciplinary range of professional services and products to target customers throughout Europe in order to deliver increased value for both our shareholders and the customers that we serve. We have seen pressure on our profits and a squeeze on returns in this competitive market with several new entrants to our market offering aggressive price reductions in some of our core areas. Given the extraordinary market conditions, the Board has taken the decision to make some important changes.

In order to protect margins we are announcing the appointment of a new European Director of Operations, John Taylor, who will be responsible for reviewing operational delivery and protecting margins across the region. John will be bringing on board a new team to support him through these challenging times.

Fact and fiction: how the brain responds

These are two very different stories. Or are they? In both stories a group of people face a challenge, a leader takes action and others are asked to support in making a change. Both stories are written to communicate something important to the audience. Both are designed to educate and inform. Both are a call to action. So why do we have such different responses and emotions when we read them? Why is only one story easy to remember? And what can neuroscience tell us about what's happening inside our brain when we read these stories?

Our brain on fiction

When we're presented with information there are two main areas in our brain that light up: Wernicke's area and Broca's area. The business story uses information, abstract concepts and facts while 'The Orchestra of Recycled Parts' uses sensory-specific language.

The first story starts with a setting we can relate to, it's set in a small town called Catuera in Paraguay. Immediately, stored memories associated with the geography and culture of Latin America are activated and start to build a rich multidimensional image in the brain, somewhat like a movie. We imagine what the people might look like – their features, hair colour, clothes. Then the story moves on to describe the setting in rich, sensory-specific language: *'bin liners that overflow with household waste'*; *'flies and stench';* *instruments forged from the city's rubbish'*; *'a violin made out of recycled parts'*. As we read, multiple brain regions are engaged including the sensory cortex and cerebellum associated with processing texture and sensation (e.g. *'headscarves that protect them from the high sun'*); the motor cortex when we read about physical movement (e.g *'race towards a rubbish truck'*, *'practising two hours a day'*), the olfactory cortex for smell, or memories of smells (*'flies and stench'*), the visual cortex for colour and shape (*'hands black with dirt'*, *'the high sun'*) and the auditory cortex for sound. If you've heard Pachelbel's Canon your brain's auditory cortex may start to silently recall musical fragments. Thus internally generated mental representations evoked by language can have a flavour similar to the real experience. This story engages multiple brain regions in order to build and shape our emotional and cognitive response. As we read, we quickly begin to feel as if what's happening *out there* is actually happening *in here*.

But the most powerful thing about that story is its ability to evoke a complex range of emotions because it's a deeply human story that connects to the lives of others. The story takes us through many of the seven core emotions including touching on two emotions that are often excluded in many stories: disgust (the rubbish dump, flies, stench) and surprise (instruments made out of old rubbish and children who can play one of the most famous pieces of classical music on such rudimentary instruments). Surprise is generated by an unusual twist in the story which challenges our expectations, and this is a novelty the brain loves. Surprise holds our attention for longer precisely because the outcome is unknown – it could be positive or negative and we need to maintain our attention to check which it is. In this story, the conclusion that beautiful music is made out of the stench and rubbish is a pleasant surprise.

Every rich sensory image, sound, texture, colour, sensation and emotion provides a *hook* for our brain as the story draws us in and maintains our attention effortlessly in a multisensory experience. This is the power of a great story. The evocative story above is mapped out in the brain image given in Fig. 5.1. Sensory cortices are activated as the richness of the story is processed, creating a mental representation of visual images (visual cortex), smells (olfactory cortex), memories (arising from the hippocampus and limbic system) and even representations related to the motoric aspects of playing a musical instrument or picking through garbage (motor cortex). All these representations are co-ordinated by the frontal lobe, which maintains attention on the story as it is built up, decides where to focus attention and inhibits other processing, as well as keeping in mind all the rich imagery. This whole brain experience makes it easy to remember the story.

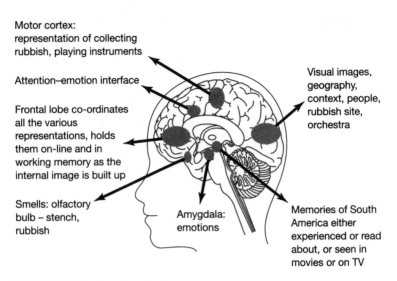

Motor cortex:
representation of collecting
rubbish, playing instruments

Attention–emotion interface

Frontal lobe co-ordinates
all the various
representations, holds
them on-line and in
working memory as the
internal image is built up

Smells: olfactory
bulb – stench,
rubbish

Amygdala:
emotions

Visual images,
geography,
context, people,
rubbish site,
orchestra

Memories of South
America either
experienced or read
about, or seen in
movies or on TV

FIGURE 5.1 Our brain on fiction.

Our brain on facts and information

When we are listening to the corporate story, there is very little sensory information to trigger memories, sensory imagery or representations. Rather the basics of the language network are activated as we listen and attempt to process the meaning of the information. Typically, Wernicke's area is activated as we try to comprehend and take meaning out of the information we are encoding (see Fig. 5.2) – but there is not very much else going on.

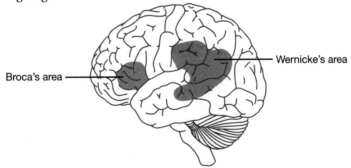

Broca's area

Wernicke's area

FIGURE 5.2 Our brain on fact.

In the business story, we understand there's a problem, but we don't really know what it is. The language is abstract so there's very little sensory-specific images for the brain to hook on to and recall later – we're suspended in a frustrating cognitive guessing game. The story feels disembodied, out of time and out of place. We know there's a person called John Taylor but that's it. There's little energy or interest in the story, there's no surprises and few images come to mind (no colour, texture, smell or sound).

Language that slips and language that sticks in the brain

Business language	Narrative language
Abstract, conceptual, facts, figures, data, jargon, information heavy.	Colourful, descriptive, sensory-specific language, that engages the senses.
Unemotional and 'cold' language.	Emotional language that generates strong emotional memories.
No personality. Indistinct. Could be written by any corporate company.	Has loads of personality and uniqueness.
Tends to feel 'out of time and place'.	Creates a rich sense of time and place.
Does not motivate action in the mind of the audience.	Motivates action through the use of emotion.
Exclusive – leaves people out.	Inclusive – invites everyone in.
Uses the restricted language (jargon) of the 'in-group' and excludes people 'outside' the group.	Uses universal language of communication. Stories that can be shared across cultures.
There's no clear, central message.	The message is clear, distinct and compelling.

▶

Business language	Narrative language
Needs to be read slowly. The brain trips over sentences. Re-reading is often required.	Effortless reading. The brain connects to the story quickly and easily.
Instantly forgettable and almost impossible to summarise into bite-sized chunks. Slips out of the mind.	Unforgettable, could be summarised and retold to others weeks, months or years after hearing. Sticks in the mind.

1st rule of influence through storytelling:

Share your passion by telling a passionate story. Talk about real people, in real situations, facing real challenges to emotionally engage with the audience.

The science of persuasion

Companies spend billions a year on advertising because it works and advertising is storytelling. Children's products use memorable cartoon characters with product personalities that children identify with: lions, tigers, monkeys, birds, superman, Disney characters and characters such as the Milky Bar Kid. The most successful and memorable adverts are those that tell the best stories and spark emotional connection and personal identification with the product.

One of the most famous British ad campaigns of all time was the Gold Blend advertisements which started in 1987. The campaign was originally designed as three commercials that would tell a short story about a young couple who met by chance and fell in love, but it was so successful that it ended up running 11 adverts for nearly nine years. The success of the campaign led the advertising company to 'advertise' the date and time when the next commercial in the series would be shown, and one of the last of the adverts drew over 30 million viewers in the UK. Jennifer Edson Escales, a marketing researcher at Vanderbuilt University, found that a test audience had more positive reactions to advertisements that were told as narratives than those which used facts and arguments. This is critical for anyone who wants to persuade, especially businesses who tend to focus on persuading through 'information'.

Have you ever been to a presentation where you are given statistics, percentages and facts over and over? It often raises more questions in the mind of the audience, such as: 'How valid is the data?' Too many facts move the brain into analytic mode. Use compelling facts in your message, but support them by telling stories that bring them to life and act as hooks.

Let's look at the differences between how the brain processes stories and information.

Messages that stick and messages that slip

The neuroscience of storytelling	The neuroscience of information
Stories activate multi-sensory cortices; motor, auditory, olfactory, somatosensory and visual.	Information mainly activates Broca's and Wernicke's area.
Stories use sensory-specific words which are easier for the brain to imagine and then elaborate on. Each person will have their own unique imaginative experience generated from these associations.	Information uses abstract, conceptual language that is more difficult for the brain to find associated sensory images.

▶

The neuroscience of storytelling	The neuroscience of information
Great stories are easily recalled due to the power of their sensory associations.	Information is difficult for the brain to record and remember, (which is why we use acronyms and other recall devices to help us remember).
Characters in stories generate emotional associations and we can identify with the character.	We don't identify with information.
Great stories are *always* emotional.	Information is devoid of emotion.
Stories have recognisable structure: beginning, middle and end, which is familiar to the brain.	Information is more linear.
Stories motivate us to move away from or toward something. These responses are deeply embedded in the brain as motivational drives.	Information is not inherently motivational unless knowing about something has an additional benefit to us in terms of our ability to survive or thrive.

2nd rule of influence through storytelling:

Emotion trumps facts when it comes to persuasion and influence.

Stories simplify complexity

The story of the monkey and the ice-cream that is used in Chapter 2 is not completely accurate, but it's become a commonly quoted story in many books and articles on the discovery of mirror neurons. Even the neuroscientist Marco Iacoboni had this to say about it:

One of the numerous stories going around the world of science holds that Vittorio Gallese was licking an ice-cream cone in the lab when a neuron wired in the macaque's brain started firing. I heard this story several times in several places, and at some point I started believing it myself. In fact, I became one of the vehicles for transmitting this meme, because I told the ice-cream story in seminars and even to some journalists interviewing me about mirror neurons.... Alas, it turns out that the ice-cream story is not true at all ... but it is charming and has proved to be an appealing and tenacious story, both to tell and to hear.

(Iacoboni, M, *Mirroring People*, 2009, p. 52)

Perhaps the reason the story is so tenacious in the press and online is because it condenses a complex scientific journey over many years with all of the essential and (correct) elements woven into a simple and memorable story that can be passed on from one person to the next. For the purpose of sharing the scientific journey with the public in an instantly memorable form the story is *true enough*.

3rd rule of influence through storytelling:

Great stories activate multi-sensory networks – sights, sounds, texture, colour and emotion – to prime a detailed internal representation in the minds of the audience. This makes them easy to recall.

Managing change

Telling the story of change

Since the global financial crisis, many businesses have been restructuring: managing mergers and acquisitions, consolidations, outsourcing and adapting to the new economic realities of austerity and globalisation. For every company, long-term success depends on how well they adapt to a new economic and political environment. Yet a staggering 70 per cent of all change programmes fail to achieve what they set out to do (Michael Beer and Nitin Norhia, 2000, Cracking the code of change). That's a huge waste of time, energy and money and means that only 30 per cent of companies will build the strongest possible platform for success.

So what's gone wrong? Why are so many smart people failing to deliver effective change? Most businesses are traditionally built on 'left-brain' thinking with logic, rationality, facts, data, ratios and information dominating decision-making and communication. While left-brain thinking is critical in decision-making and problem-solving, it tends to drown out the important role storytelling plays in helping employees successfully navigate change and understand complex issues. If emotion rather than logic is really the driving force of so many of our decisions, then stories are the best way to share and build emotional connection. For years CEOs have learnt to tell the *information* story; but few CEOs have learned how to tell the *inspiration* story. But it's not only important for CEOs; we are all in positions of leadership in some areas of our life and we often need to tell a story that inspires others – as a manager of a team, running our own business, or in our community or social groups.

4th rule of influence through storytelling:

Storytelling is inherently a leadership skill that serves us in all areas of our life.

How our brain responds to stress

For employees, the announcement of a major restructure is the modern equivalent of seeing a predator size you up for lunch, an experience which launches a primitive, automatic 'fight–flight' response. The brain's response to threat is to activate the amygdala which releases the stress hormones cortisol and adrenaline into the blood. Under threat, we go into a fight, flight or freeze response; our heart rate increases, blood rushes to our extremities and our attention shifts to focus on what we need to do to survive. For centuries our response to threat has tended to be short-lived; we either survive or we're lunch.

But in today's business world, we often experience the same reaction to things that are not life-threatening (change, restructure, redundancy) but that have the same physiological punch. Given that large-scale change in most organisations takes weeks, months (or sometimes years) and that change seems to be a constant, many employees can experience an almost constant low-level amygdala hijack while waiting to find out whether or not their job is safe.

The effects of increased levels of cortisol and adrenaline in the body are to reduce the brain's capacity for creative thinking and problem-solving and to compromise the body's immune system and sleep patterns. Many employees withdraw their focus from the projects they are working on while they wait to find out how the change will affect budgets, timescales, programmes, investments and priorities. The mantra of leaders is often: 'continue to do exactly what you are doing until told otherwise', but the brain's response to increased uncertainty and a reduced sense of control maintains amygdala activity in a way that compromises cognitive functioning (see Fig. 5.3).

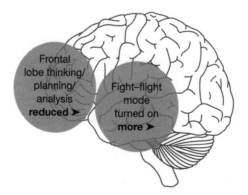

FIGURE 5.3 The effect of stress on the brain.

The brain has evolved more (and faster) circuits to detect threat than reward. Employees are in a state of chronic mild to moderate arousal as decisions about redundancy are made. Given our ability to empathise (through the mirror neuron system), it's not long before emotional contagion spreads feelings of fear and anxiety through the group. Just when companies need employees to help them reinvigorate the business, they are in a psychological holding pattern and can experience reduced focus, motivation, concentration and performance resulting from stress.

Using stories to manage change

So what can CEOs and leaders do to influence employees and help them navigate change? A leader's role is as much about managing the emotions and brains of employees as it is about managing the bottom line. CEOs can help employees make sense of the change through a clear and consistent narrative that acknowledges their emotions and connects in a psychologically congruent way.

So what's the best way to communicate with others to build understanding and emotional connection? How can you tell the story of change in a brain-friendly way? You need to do two things: talk their language and tell stories that link the past and future while acknowledging the present. Your story needs to validate emotions and then to consciously support emotional processing within the group to facilitate healthy growth and change.

Denominalise

Start by unpacking the word *change* and turning it back into the verb *changing*. Be clear about what specifically needs to change – when, where, how and why. Give clear, sensory-specific examples of what the change entails, find examples or stories of real people in the business who will manage the change. Own the decisions and take responsibility.

Think about the difference between these two statements. How does each statement make you feel?

➡ The leadership has decided to downsize the business in order to improve profitability.

➡ I have taken the difficult decision to review our headcount in the light of our poor financial results. As leaders, we will do everything in our power to minimise the impact on employees.

Think about the emotional and psychological impact of the language you use. Put people at the heart of your story and ensure leaders are visible and accountable.

Toward and away from

Change is always about moving *away from* what is familiar and *toward* an unknown future. Talk about both motivational emotions in your communication. Grieving and letting go is a critical aspect of transitioning into a different future. It's important to honour the past because many employees may have been in the company for years. A successful future can only be built on a successful past. Bring what's good and important from the company's vision into the future while letting go of what no longer serves the business.

5th rule of influence through storytelling:

Help people deal with change by contextualising: What's happened and why? Where are we going next? What will it look like when we get there?

The emotional chain

Leaders who are able to talk about the emotional impact of change build credibility and empathy with employees. The temptation is to use the default 'left-brain' response in a 'right-brain' situation (to respond to powerful emotions with logic and by appealing to people's rational brain).

When the fight–flight response is activated, our frontal lobe closes down which compromises our ability to make decisions, forward plan and respond flexibly. If the brain thinks we're about to be eaten by a tiger, we don't need to plan our summer holiday or consider all the different ways we can contribute in the organisation. We think about what we need to do to survive. Under threat, our limbic system is turned ON and our frontal lobe is turned OFF (see Fig. 5.4).

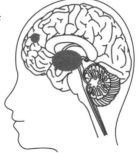

- Limbic ON
- Frontal OFF

FIGURE 5.4 The brain under stress.

Leaders occupy a powerful and influential role as the head of the group and employees look to leaders to model appropriate responses to change. When leaders are comfortable talking about the emotional challenges evoked by change, they generate emotional resonance with their audience and show empathy, insight and understanding. The transition curve (see Fig. 5.5) illuminates the emotional response over time to change. The skillful leader meets employees where they are. It would be unreasonable to expect acceptance and integration of the change when the group is still in the shock, anger or denial phase.

As you design each communication, think about how you can actively validate the emotions of employees. The model in Figure 5.5 shows the emotional cycle and how emotions need to be processed sequentially from negative through to the more neutral emotions and finally to the positive emotions as the organisation moves back into a steady state. Take time to acknowledge each stage fully.

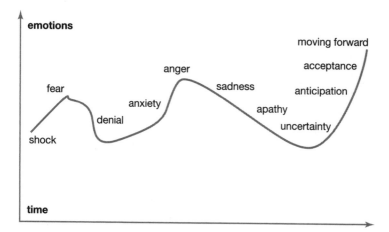

FIGURE 5.5 Transition curve.

Storytelling framework to shift emotions

Emotions	Begin the change – storylines
Denial, anger, anxiety, sadness, depression	Talk about these openly and acknowledge the difficulty of change and the feelings people experience when facing change. Use the change curve in your communications as a way to normalise the experience of employees. Once people can label what they feel, they can begin to manage these powerful derailing emotions.
Story themes: threat and challenge	Share some of the challenges faced by the senior team in coming to final decisions and reassure people that these have been made with a great deal of thought and consideration.
Pride, acknowledge the past	Acknowledge the successes of the past and the fact that employees have already helped to overcome challenges in the past.
Story themes: history and shared values and experiences	Once you acknowledge the past, you can acknowledge the problems and issues that need to change.
Motivated, energised and committed to support change	Talk about the problems and challenges and involve employees in designing the solutions to direct energy towards change.
Story themes: renewal and regeneration	Talk about what the future looks like and describe the steps you need to take to get there. Create compelling pictures of the future.

Toward emotions	Moving through the change – storylines
Reassurance, respect, acknowledgement, safe to express emotions during time of uncertainty	Tell stories about an uncertain future. Nothing is set. Unless we get everybody involved, even the best plan may still fail. It takes the whole community to make this work. Spend time telling the story of progress and be honest about the challenges involved. When people are involved in the change they will be motivated and energised to support it.
Story themes: overcoming, leaving and return	Leaders have knowledge, resources and skills, but they cannot see all of the details and this is where change can fail. How can employees help to make sure that the big picture and details are managed together? The group changes *together* – this is an opportunity for employees to contribute ideas, solutions and creative ideas.

Toward emotions	New beginnings – storylines
Excitement, anticipation, energised, involved, included, valued, appreciated	Celebrate progress and success all the way through. Show the change curve and celebrate the resilience of employees to get through the change. Acknowledge efforts, ideas and contributions. Focus on public recognition and create symbolic moments where people can be together to reconnect.
Story themes: new beginnings, journey and return	Look back on the change once it's over and use it in the future to talk about how the group faced a challenge and overcame it. Use it as a positive story to generate feelings of pride, achievement and survival.

Emotions sell – everything

Few companies understand the role emotions play in determining our choices better than consumer brands who spend millions of dollars to create deep and often unconscious emotional associations between consumers and their brands. Global companies such as Google, CBS, Frito-Lay and Coca-Cola are investing in a new field of marketing called neuromarketing to study people's brain activity and biometrics (heart rate and respiratory rate) in response to marketing stimuli. Some have built in-house laboratories and employed their own neuroscientists to find out how consumer choice can be influenced by emotional responses to brands and products. And one of the most commonly used marketing strategies is to 'prime' a positive emotional response to a brand in the minds of consumers.

But what is priming and how can if affect us without us even knowing? Priming is the ability to create an implicit memory that will influence a later response to a stimulus – advertising is a conscious form of priming because consumers often choose one particular product over another because they've been exposed to an advertisement which makes the product more 'familiar' and therefore more trusted. But companies also look to prime emotional associations by placing their products in TV shows and movies so that the product takes on an unconscious emotional connection with a popular or much-loved actor. The size of endorsement fees paid to famous sports people is directly in proportion to their ability to prime a particular emotional response in consumers to the brand of the corporate sponsor. The US golfer, Tiger Woods, has made over $1 billion in earnings, a large proportion of which is made up of sponsorship and endorsement fees. When Nike wanted to build its golfing brand, it was Tiger Woods' endorsement that saw the Nike brand grow from a start-up to the leading golf clothing and equipment company in the world – now worth more than $600 million in sales.

If our brains are wired to make choices based on the strength of our emotional associations then the companies that succeed in creating the most compelling emotions win. Coca-Cola's tagline *Open Happiness* sums up the way many global brands seek to create a specific neural association between a product and a particular emotion, and few companies understand the power of selling emotion, better than Coca-Cola. In fact it's been so successful that it could be seen as selling emotion over and above even taste.

Case study

In a famous study undertaken in 2004, 67 people underwent brain scanning while taking a blind taste test for both Coca-Cola and Pepsi. When subjects were unaware of the brand they were drinking, half of them chose the taste of Pepsi over Coke; the part of their brain which was activated was the ventromedial prefrontal cortex, a region that processes feelings of reward. But once the subjects were told when they were drinking Coke, 75 per cent said that it tasted better. So what could explain their change of mind? The researchers found that once the subjects knew which brand they were drinking their brain scans showed increased activity in the lateral prefrontal cortex, which is an area of the brain that governs high level cognition, as well as the hippocampus which is an area related to memory.

Source: McClure, S M *et al*. (2004) Neural correlates of behavioral preference for culturally familiar drinks.

The decision to choose Coke was influenced by deeper emotional memories and associations built up over years through advertising that primes positive unconscious emotional responses that override taste alone. The largest proportion of Coca-Cola's marketing spend is concentrated over summer holidays and Christmas, two of the most iconic times of the year when most consumers spend time with loved ones celebrating, relaxing and having fun. If our brain selects memories based on the *strongest emotion* and Coke has invested billions over many years advertising at these peak emotional moments in our lives, it's not surprising that it has succeeded in dominating the cola market in the minds of consumers. Dr Read Montague said: *'We live in a sea of cultural images ... Everybody has heard of Coke and Pepsi, they have messages, and ... those messages have insinuated themselves in our nervous system'* (quoted in http://news.bbc.co.uk/1/hi/health/3739462.stm).

Exercise

Try it out for yourself – notice your own mental and emotional associations with ideas of 'Christmas' or summer holidays.

Sit quietly for a moment and close your eyes. Say the words to yourself and, as you do so, pay close attention to any images, feelings, other thoughts and words or memories that come into your mind.

Notice the rich associations, emotions, images and memories with these words.

Emotions drive decisions

Another neuroscientist who is interested in the role emotions play in decision-making is Drew Weston who argues in his 2007 book *The Political Brain,* that the US Republican Party dominates the key policy debates because they have developed a political language that generates powerful emotions in the minds of voters whereas the Democrats have traditionally relied on appealing to voter's rational thinking (p. 175). Drew Weston and his team conducted a series of experiments with Republican and Democrat partisans to find out what would happen when they experienced a conflict between what they emotionally wanted to believe and what was factually true. While scanning their brains in a functional magnetic resonance imaging machine, the participants were presented with an initial statement from a candidate followed by a contradictory statement. For example, Bush supporters were given the following statements:

Statement One: Bush supporters

'Having been here and seeing the care that these troops get is comforting for me and Laura. We must provide the best care for anybody who is willing to put their life in harm's way for our country.'
George Bush

Statement Two: Bush supporters

Mr Bush's visit came on the same day that the administration announced its immediate cut-off of VA hospital access to approximately 164 000 veterans.

Democratic supporters were faced with a similar challenge with an initial statement made by John Kerry during the Gulf War when writing to a constituent:

Statement One: Kerry supporters

'Thank you for contacting me to express your opposition ... I share your concerns. I voted in favour of a resolution that would have insisted that economic sanctions be given more time to work.'
John Kerry

This was followed by a statement Kerry made seven days later when he wrote to a different constituent saying:

Statement Two: Kerry supporters

'Thank you for expressing your support for the Iraqi invasion of Kuwait. From the outset of the invasion, I have strongly and unequivocally supported President Bush's response to the crisis.'

John Kerry

What's interesting about Drew's research is that while both Democrats and Republicans were able to see the contradiction of the other party's statement, they were unable to see the contradiction in what their own candidate said. The brain scans revealed that when participants read the contradictory statement from their own party, a network of neurons were activated that produced emotional distress. In an attempt to reduce the distress, participants chose to 'ignore' the source of the distress through faulty reasoning. Drew says that: *'In politics, when reason and emotion collide, emotion invariably wins. Although the marketplace of ideas is a great place to shop for policies, the marketplace that matters most in American politics is the* **marketplace of emotions***'* (p. 35). He goes on to say that *'The data from political science are crystal clear: people vote for the candidate who elicits the right feelings, not the candidate who presents the best arguments'* (p. 125).

6th rule of influence through storytelling:

Emotions drive our decisions.

Your story in a nutshell

Sometimes we need to develop a clear, simple story with a big emotional punch. We may have limited time at a meeting or presentation or limited space on a website or promotional document, but we still need to get our message across and we need it to stick. We want to sell an idea in a nutshell. Let's look at who tells the best short stories and what can we learn from them.

Company taglines are a great way to think about how you might create a simple compelling story that sticks in the mind. Taglines create specific emotional responses to the brand or product – consumers thought Coca-Cola tasted better not because of the actual taste but because of the emotional associations of the brand.

Taglines seek to create specific emotional responses in consumers by subliminally activating a rich web of images, memories and associations with 'toward' emotions driving brands like Coca-Cola and Nike (*Open Happiness* and *Just Do It*) and 'away from' emotions driving brands like Amex and Ajax (*Don't leave home without it* and *Stronger than Dirt*). These brands seek to meet our emotional needs for friendship, love, connection and adventure or security, certainty and safety. While very few companies use the emotion of fear to drive behaviour, for some organisations such as Friends of the Animals, fear is an effective motivating emotion: *Extinct is Forever*. But some of the most memorable taglines are those that use the emotion of surprise because it requires us to uncover different levels of meaning – what thoughts or feelings come to mind when you read the US Army's tagline: *Some of the best men are women*?

How do you want your reader to feel at the end of your message? What's the core emotion you want to evoke? Once you've discovered the heart of your message you can keep returning to it as your core theme and core motivational force. This exercise helps you discover the beating heart of your message and to think creatively. It's a useful primer when you are brainstorming ideas for a new product, service, message or presentation. Choose a short, punchy core idea to help communicate your ideas, focus your message and elicit the right emotional impact.

7th rule of influence through storytelling:

Summarise your story into a single compelling idea to reveal the emotional heart of your message.

Storytelling framework

The framework illustrated in Fig. 5.6 shows the elements you can use to develop your communication.

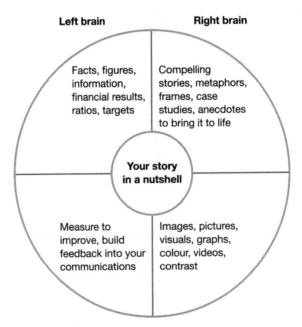

Left brain   **Right brain**

Facts, figures, information, financial results, ratios, targets

Compelling stories, metaphors, frames, case studies, anecdotes to bring it to life

Your story in a nutshell

Measure to improve, build feedback into your communications

Images, pictures, visuals, graphs, colour, videos, contrast

FIGURE 5.6 Storytelling framework – create your content.

Story in a nutshell

Sum up your key idea. What's the core of your message? What's the single most important thing you want your audience to understand and remember? Once you have summarised the story into a core (emotional) idea, you have the perfect hook that will help you stay on track and around which you can focus the rest of your information.

Left brain

What are the facts, figures and information that support your core idea? What are the important proof points that your audience need to know? You might change the mix of storytelling and facts depending on your audience; financially literate senior people will want more financial information than employees. So change your blend to match your audience.

Right brain

What are the emotions of the audience when you start? Where do you want to move them from and where do you want them to go emotionally? How will your story help to motivate and inspire people?

Increase your influence by measuring

Get feedback and find out what works well for your audience. Build measurement into your communication as a surefire way to help you improve: this is one of the habits of influential communicators. Here are some methods for getting feedback from your audience.

➡ Ask people to complete a short questionnaire at the end of the event for instant feedback.
➡ Send people a link to an online survey after the event (perhaps with a compelling summary and promotional opportunity).

➡ Speak to people after a presentation or talk and get personal feedback.

➡ Ask a trusted advisor for honest feedback and for tips on what you could do better next time.

➡ If you are in a corporate communication function, hold focus groups with employees to get in-depth feedback and use this as an opportunity to get their input about what works for them.

➡ Work with senior managers to measure whether the investment in their communication helps to improve the business, increase customer satisfaction or increase the motivation and engagement of employees.

➡ Design an annual online employee survey to measure and track your communications on a regular basis and use this as part of your annual communications planning.

➡ Ask your customers how well you are doing and how they rate your ability to sell to and serve them.

Pictures and images

There's a saying that a picture tells a thousand words – well it's true. Use powerful images to support your message. If you are delivering a presentation, or formal speech, use a range of support materials to help you tell your story and help shift the emotions in the room. You might want to include great videos or powerful emotional images, photos or music to generate positive emotions in your audience. Spend as much time preparing emotional content as you do data and information.

8th rule of influence through storytelling:

Use pictures to support your ideas and give the audience visual anchors to remember your message.

Brain Rules:

1. Emotional stories are sticky and help us retain and recall information.

2. Stories have a familiar framework that provide a clear structure we understand and remember.

3. The brain is more likely to challenge facts and data but to accept the 'truth' of narrative.

4. Major change is experienced as a threat to survival: the amygdala triggers our fight–flight or freeze response so consciously manage the emotions involved in change.

5. Continued uncertainty maintains this emotional reaction and its psychological and physiological effects.

6. Employees withdraw emotional energy to focus on their own survival.

7. Constant low-level amygdala hijack prevents the brain from thinking clearly, reduces problem-solving and stifles creativity.

Top Tips:

1. Put emotions at the heart of your story.

2. Use plain, simple, sensory-specific language.

3. Use frames and metaphors to help explain business or technical concepts.

4. Use visual images to elicit emotions and motivate the audience to action.

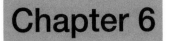

Chapter 6

Influence in every channel

I have no special talents, I am only passionately curious.

Albert Einstein

Increase your influence – become even more curious

Influential people are insatiably curious about others; they make a habit of noticing how they think, feel and decide. Their attention is tuned in to notice, to question and to learn. Curiosity is a bedrock skill of influence and persuasion. When you are deeply curious about how to best approach an opportunity, learn from a setback or face a challenge you will rapidly increase your knowledge, emotional resilience and creative ideas; all ingredients of influence.

In an experiment designed to look at the brain science of curiosity, George Loewenstein and his team scanned subjects with fMRI while they read trivia questions. They discovered that when the subjects were in a state of being curious they had increased activity in the caudate, the prefrontal cortex and the gyri areas of the brain. It's the caudate that sits at the intersection of new knowledge and positive emotion and is closely linked to parts of the dopamine reward pathway – in other words, curiosity is like a reward for the brain and it's rooted in the same neural pathway that responds to sex, drugs and rock 'n' roll.

Source: Kang, M J *et al*. (2009) The wick in the candle of learning: epistemic curiosity activates reward circuitry and enhances memory.

We need to influence people through many different channels – on the phone, face to face, in formal presentations or sales pitches – and each channel has its own unique challenges and opportunities. So once we become curious about how we can do things differently in whatever channel we use to communicate with others we can choose the right channel and make sure we use it to our best advantage.

1st rule of influence in every channel:

Become curious about how you can be even more persuasive and influential.

The problem with email and how to fix it

There's a whole world out there (mostly online) where scientists, psychologists, neuroscientists, technology companies, health professionals and other curious souls are talking about the effects of information overload on our brains, bodies and emotions. Most of us who sit in front of computers all day will understand what the psychiatrist Howard Hallowell means when he talks about 'attention deficit trait' – the average worker receives around 100 emails a day and managers up to 300, yet everyone agrees that a third of them are 'unnecessary'. It's no wonder knowledge workers find it difficult to stay focused given that they spend around two hours a day dealing with information that is of little or no value to them. But it's not just the amount of time wasted, it's also stressful; so stressful in fact that Linda Stone has discovered that many of us suffer from 'email apnea' (the unconscious cessation of regular and steady breathing) – a physiological response to dealing with so much information.

The cost of information overload for business is also significant: Intel's research on its own employees found that the company was wasting $1 billion a year on lost productivity alone; while HP's research found that the effect on knowledge workers who were constantly interrupted was that their IQ was reduced by up to 10 points (the equivalent to being stoned on marijuana). A study by Microsoft found that when we're interrupted by an email or phone alert we not only read the message but we take, on average, 24 minutes to return to the task we were doing. So when we add it all up, the cost to both business and us is enormous.

Many of us now use email to sell our services or products, to strengthen important relationships or to build new ones. Most projects at work are delivered by the back and forth seesaw of email traffic and instant messaging, with people who sit opposite one another emailing rather than talking. We've become addicted. But email should come with its own special health warning and, if we want to influence somebody, it is better to pick up the phone or arrange a personal meeting. If we use email to sell our ideas and persuade others we need to get to grips with what's really happening in this slippery medium because one of the most important recent research findings on email is that it's been proven to have an inbuilt *negative bias*. If you send an email you think is 'positive', the message is received by the other person as 'neutral', but when you send an email that is 'neutral', it is likely to be read in a more negative light. Given that it's often used to deliver messages we might find difficult to deliver face-to-face, email can become a heat-seeking missile for misunderstanding and reducing our influence with others.

I can't see you – I can't read your intention

We've spent thousands of years developing a mirror neuron system that is sophisticated enough to read the subtle physical and verbal cues that help us interpret another person's intention, but email strips us of all of these which makes it easy to misread other people's intention (and for them to misunderstand ours). Someone might send us a short email because they are busy and under pressure but, if we are under stress or hoping for a different response, then it's easy to read into it a more negative intention. And when we need a quick decision or response, as each day passes we begin to wonder: 'Did they receive it?', 'Has it been lost in the spam box?', 'Have they actually read it? Perhaps they missed it and it's now buried, unread under hundreds of new emails?' Soon we wonder whether we should send a follow-up email, but will that come across as pushy? Perhaps they're out of the office but didn't turn their reminder on? Or perhaps they are ignoring us after all. The list goes on and on. Our brain runs a tracker system to remember all the email threads that are still waiting for replies or action, or next steps. This all takes cognitive space and time and is a huge distraction to getting down to what's really important.

And remember that sometimes it's you whose email may be having this effect on others. The table below gives some advice for effective use of email.

RESPECT – Detox your email	
Reduce	Reduce the amount of emails you send – try to kick the habit one email at a time Reduce the people you copy in (only those who absolutely, positively need to know) Reduce your anxiety about answering each email as it comes in – turn on your email at set times of the day rather than having email 'always on'
Exercise	Exercise your legs – clear your mind on the way to the other person's desk, take ten deep breaths and recharge your brain Exercise your brain – speak to your colleagues, customers and suppliers whenever you can Exercise restraint in all thing email
Shorten	Shorten the length of your email Become famous for sending the clearest and most succinct emails
Phone	Phone your friends, customers and colleagues when someone needs a quick response, information or advice to build rapport Phone your boss and colleagues to get decisions quickly – avoid the paralysis caused by waiting for multiple decisions from others
Eliminate	Eliminate jargon, preamble, formality, length, complexity, blind copies, copies, storing, failing to reply
Cut out	Cut out clutter, compexity and long email trails Cut out hiding behind email when you have bad news to tell – always do this face to face
Think	Think about making email more positive given the negative bias rule Think about the receiver at all times Think about using structure to simplify and make clearer Think about the impact of every email you send

2nd rule of influence in every channel:

Email has been proven to have a negative bias. That's a red light for influence. Use it sparingly and then make it even more positive.

Tips for email influence:

1. Create a clear, succinct subject heading so the receiver understands purpose, actions and any timelines they need to meet.

2. Use structure to create clarity: bullet points, summaries.

3. The shorter the better.

4. List actions in a box at the top of the email.

5. Take a minimum of 24 hours before you respond to an email that made you angry or upset. If possible, telephone or meet face to face to resolve the issue.

6. Send detailed information on paper, or arrange a short meeting or telephone call.

Turbo-charge your meetings

We often set regular meetings on the same day, with the same people for the same length of time and often with the same agenda so it's easy to fall into the trap of repeating the same structure and the same behaviours. The problem is we get the same outcomes. Here are some of the typical problems of ineffective meetings:

➡ Unclear outcomes, purpose or agenda.

➡ Inviting everyone in the team rather than those who need to attend.

➡ Thinking meetings are a way to build team spirit.

→ Starting late, overrunning, allowing people to waffle.

→ Holding meetings that are little more than a way to update the team on activities.

The first thing to do is to be clear and distinguish between each meeting you have – agree the purpose and what specifically you want to achieve. First, consider what type of meeting you need to hold. The most common type of business meeting is a 'telling' meeting where people present an update on their specific area to the rest of the team; these are the least effective meetings you can hold. Meetings should be focused on getting people to take action, to make decisions or to contribute their ideas about a project, plan or proposal. So the first step is to be clear about the purpose of your meeting. The table below describes four different types of team meeting and their outcomes in terms of behaviour.

Telling	Thinking
Meetings to 'download' one-way information. Everybody takes turns to tell the other team members what they've been doing.	Ad-hoc meeting to get people's best thinking to solve a problem, challenge, design a new project, or discuss a new opportunity.
Behaviour: People feel emotionally disconnected and switch off. A distraction from demanding work. People feel 'pressured' to attend.	**Behaviour**: People feel energised, important, consulted. A clear purpose for the discussion. People feel motivated to attend.
One-way download, siloed thinking and behaviour.	**Two-way, collaborative, insightful.**
Invite: All team members.	**Invite: Those who can contribute from all parts of the business.**

Collaborating	Deciding
Meeting to co-ordinate activities on projects, proposals, activities.	Ad-hoc meeting to make important decisions for the business. This is a true leadership team meeting.
Behaviour: People are pragmatic and update the team on progress and align activities. People feel motivated to attend.	**Behaviour**: People are focused on critical decisions. People feel responsible for outcomes.
Two-way, consultative, co-ordinating tasks.	**Two-way, decision-making, strategic.**
Invite: Project team members only.	**Invite: Decision-makers only.**

3rd rule of influence in every channel:

For meetings, decide which type of meeting you need to hold first.

The first thing to do is to get your team to agree what's working well and what needs to change and watch their motivation and commitment increase. Work through these questions with your team:

➡ Are meetings the best structure to achieve our shared goals?

➡ What other structures would work better for us?

➡ What would an ideal meeting be like?

➡ What should we stop doing at meetings?

➡ What is not working well in our meetings?

➡ What's the most important thing we should be discussing at our meetings?

➡ What do we want by the end of the meeting that we don't have now?

➡ What will we each do before our next meeting to stay on track?

➡ What has been the most useful thing we have achieved today?

Seven ways to ignite your meetings

Here are seven strategies to make your meetings more effective in achieving their goals.

1. Frame each agenda item as a question. Ask people to prepare a one-minute response on each agenda item to activate thinking before the meeting.

2. Frame each agenda item in a nutshell. What's the point? What's in it for them? What do you want them to do? Be as structured in meetings as you are in a presentation.

3. Ask yourself what the decisions that *only this group of people* can make together are before inviting attendees. If you want to build team spirit and cohesion, hold lunch meetings for informal updates and relationship building.

4. Allocate only as much time as you need for each meeting.

5. Start on time. Stay on track. Close the meeting on time.

6. Start and end each meeting with a short appreciation. This helps people focus on solutions and puts them at ease at the start of the meeting and closes the meeting with a positive emotional boost.

4th rule of influence in every channel:

In meetings, attend to the emotional needs of participants. People thrive when they feel needed, consulted and respected.

Tips for appreciation rounds at the start and/or end of the meeting:

1. What's working well?

2. What's your most recent success?

3. What are you most proud of?

4. As a team what are we doing well?

5. What's one example of great team working?

6. If you had to sum up in one word the most positive thing, what would it be?

7. What are you most looking forward to in the next month?

(Make these very short: 30 seconds to a minute.)

Stand out from the crowd at meetings

If you want to be known as the most influential person at meetings think about the Dos and Don'ts of meeting behaviours.

Ways to lose influence in meetings	Ways to win influence in meetings
Hold regular, same time, same place, same agenda meetings and expect people to be motivated.	Think about the kind of meeting you need to hold with your team: to update people (telling) to get the best ideas (thinking), to co-ordinate project activities (collaborating) or to make critical decisions (deciding)?
Meetings that are scheduled to take place for more than an hour are unstructured, unfocused and have no clear agreed outcomes.	Make the meeting as short as possible. People are busy. People will give you high-quality focus and contribution if they know their time will be valued. You need to be very organised, focused and stick to the allotted time.
Turn up late or unprepared.	Turn up on time (or slightly early) well prepared and ready to contribute.
Ignore, deride or criticise the ideas of others.	Support the ideas of others.

▶

Disagree out of hand or without due consideration and respect for the contributor.	If you disagree, be clear, reasoned and find elements that you can include in an alternative solution.
Talk over people, interrupt or take too much time on your pet topic.	Be the best listener in the room. Listen with deep attention to everyone (not just the boss or the senior people).
Ignore or show you are uncomfortable with emotions shown by others.	Be comfortable with the emotions in the room; they are part of the group process. Acknowledge and respect the emotions of others (and your own).
Pick up phone messages, check your email, draw on your pad, keep your head down, lose focus.	Pay attention. Focus. Contribute ideas and energy.
Fail to maintain eye contact. Think about what it would be like if everyone in the room withdrew eye contact from the speaker.	Look at each person who is speaking and make eye contact. This shows you are truly listening, demonstrates interest, encouragement and builds rapport with each speaker.
Be critical or ungenerous.	Appreciate your colleagues. Thank them for their work and ideas.
Ignore or avoid debate and robust discussion.	Show that you value difference and debate. Invite debate and be comfortable with differences of opinion; it's what makes a great solution and healthy team.
Put people in an airless room with no natural light (if you have no alternative have the shortest meeting possible).	Notice the environment and ensure people are comfortable. Provide refreshments, plenty of water, fresh air (if possible) and build in enough small breaks to improve concentration and focus.

One-to-one meetings

Before every important meeting with someone you want to influence ask yourself the following questions:

➡ What does this person most value?

➡ How do they prefer to receive information – are they big picture or detail?

➡ What is their biggest concern?

➡ What do they want from me?

➡ How do they see me?

➡ Who else might be important in making this decision (if you are going to ask them for support or sign-off on a project)?

➡ What is my fallback position if I don't achieve my outcome?

➡ What's their buying strategy and how can I appeal to it?

➡ Are they motivated by what they want (toward) or what they want to avoid (away from)?

Tips for meetings

1. When you get into the room take time to establish a personal connection with the other person.

2. Be fully prepared. Bring a one-page summary as well as a more detailed report if you are unsure of exactly what they need.

3. Prepare a positive emotional state.

4. Maintain eye contact and concentration.

5. Listen, listen and then listen some more.

6. Ask incisive questions to ensure you fully understand and get all the information you need.

7. Maintain a relaxed posture, plant your feet on the floor.

8. Be clear about the next steps.

Getting things back on track

If you are meeting with somebody you've had conflict with and you want to positively influence the relationship to get back on track, use a simple but powerful neurolinguistic programming tool called metaposition. You can do the following exercise with a trusted colleague or friend or on your own.

Exercise

Go into a quiet place and step through the process below:

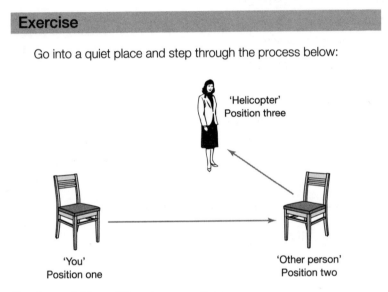

'Helicopter'
Position three

'You'
Position one

'Other person'
Position two

See the world from different perspectives.

Go to **position one** and answer the following questions from your perspective:

1. What do you want to achieve from the meeting?
2. What is most important to you about this issue (what are your values)?
3. What do you most fear?
4. How do you see the other person (judgements, criticisms, views and opinions)?
5. What beliefs do you hold?

Go to **position two** and imaginatively become the other person – use their gestures, posture and language. Talk from their perspective when answering the questions.

1. What do you want to achieve from the meeting?
2. What is most important to you about this issue (what are your values)?
3. What do you most fear?
4. How do you see the other person (judgements, criticisms, views and opinions)?
5. What beliefs do you hold?

Next move into third position, which is the neutral position, and take a moment to (imaginatively) notice the behaviour, body language, tone of voice, eye contact, energy, emotion and relationship between the two people as if you are watching them from a distance.

Go to **position three** and answer the following questions:

1. What do you notice about the way these two people interact?
2. What values do they share in common?
3. What stops them from connecting more deeply?
4. What advice would you give them to achieve their common goals?
5. What needs to change?

If you do this exercise with emotional honesty you may be surprised at what you discover. Give yourself time and space to do the exercise and reap the rewards. It can help to do it with a coach but, as long as you commit to doing the exercise 'as if' you were with a coach (avoid rushing, or assuming you already know the answer before you get there), it can uncover invaluable information that you might have missed.

The biggest challenge is to have a truly open mind about what might be going on for the other person and to be honest about your own feelings. Influence is about learning and growing, not about being 'perfect' or above the fray. The fray is where we learn and grow. Once you have gained new insights, you can then plan on how to manage the next meeting with increased influence and wisdom.

Presenting with influence

The role of mirror neurons

Have you ever sat through a presentation where the speaker was nervous, looked down, raced through their information and avoided eye contact? Chances are that you ended up feeling uncomfortable because your mirror neuron system picked up their feelings of anxiety and you began to mirror those exact same emotions (see Fig. 6.1). Feelings of fear are transmitted instantaneously from person to person and our automatic response to fear is to flee. So people literally want to get away from presenters who arouse a state of fear in them.

Unless a presenter can manage their own emotional state and get back on track, it's not long before an audience begins to actively dislike them because they are unconsciously creating unpleasant feelings in the group. And it doesn't matter how interesting or compelling the information in your presentation is, if your audience feels uncomfortable or anxious they won't concentrate on your message – they will move into fight–flight mode which will prevent their brain from thinking and motivate them to move away. And the problem with mirror neurons is that they operate on a two-way feedback loop; once the audience becomes anxious, embarrassed or uncomfortable, the presenter will pick up their emotions, which will only increase their own. This can soon turn into a full-blown, emotional downward spiral.

Fear of public speaking is one of the most common fears we all share. It's not that the best speakers have no anxiety – it's just that they spend more time preparing their emotional state. Influential speakers are influential not because of the content of their material but because of their ability to spark positive emotions in the audience.

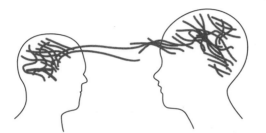

FIGURE 6.1 Our mirror neuron system helps us identify and understand the emotions of others.

5th rule of influence in every channel:

In presentations, your mirror neurons will communicate your emotions to others. Create a positive emotional state.

Delivering the message

So what are some strategies to help you deliver your message with ease and comfort and give yourself the best chance to persuade and influence?

Start with ease

The first few minutes can be the hardest as you warm up and get comfortable. Script your first 60–90 seconds so you know exactly what you want to say. Practise in front of the mirror. Record it on your phone and listen back to yourself. Memory recall research has found that we remember the first and last thing people say and not as much from the middle. So prepare a tightly structured introduction and conclusion where you sum up the main points that you want people to remember.

Be measured with your time

Make sure you have clear pauses between your sentences. When you pause, take a deep breath which will help settle your nerves and create a sense of calm. Getting off to a clear start will help you relax.

Use your audience to help you relax

Presenters who are nervous often avoid looking directly at the audience; instead they look at the back of the room, down at the floor or at the presentation slides. But this can make them appear disconnected and uninterested in their audience. When we make direct eye contact with people, this helps calm our fight–flight response – because rather than looking at a sea of people we start looking at individuals.

Make the right amount of eye contact

We all want to be seen by others and eye contact is the quickest way to acknowledge someone's presence and thereby establish empathy and rapport.

Hold eye contact for *three seconds* before moving on to the next person. This is important; less than three seconds and it feels like a cursory glance, more than three seconds and it can start to feel like a stare which triggers our fight–flight response. You can try this out in a neutral situation like at a pub or supermarket or with friends before trying this at a formal presentation to get comfortable and practise. Make it your goal to connect with as many people as you can. We all want to be seen by others and eye contact is the quickest way to acknowledge someone's presence and thereby establish empathy and rapport.

Use visually beautiful and compelling images

This is so easy to do – images are not just visual cues they're emotional cues and they can help you create positive emotions in the audience. When you change the slide, give your audience a quiet moment to look at the image, take a moment to pause and look around the room, take a deep breath and prepare your next point.

Pause

Build pauses into your presentation – a moment of silence helps to calm down anxiety, reset your focus and give your audience time to digest the information.

Use video to support your message

There are so many fascinating, educational and inspiring videos on the Internet, particularly on sites such as TED.com. Find a short clip that will help reinforce your message. Our brain loves variety and when we provide information in different ways this helps the audience remember the message, connect emotionally and gives you a chance to breath, relax and prepare.

Create two-way conversations

Create opportunities for the audience to ask questions or spend a few minutes talking to the person next to them. There are many creative ways of breaking up the talk and connecting people. Think creatively about what you want to achieve and give yourself permission to find different ways to achieve it. Stand out from the crowd by making your presentations different.

Ask yourself:

➡ How can I create a sense of ease in myself and the audience?

➡ What are some creative ways that I can get my message across?

➡ What would work best in this context?

➡ What state is my audience in and how can I move them emotionally to where I want to go?

Use timelines

We each have 'timelines' – a cognitive way of sorting time (past from future) and 'locating' things such as events, memories of the past and pictures and imaginings of the future. The majority of people locate past events to their left. For example, if you ask somebody to recall an event that happened six months ago, they will instinctively move their eyes (while they are visualising) to their left. And when asked to imagine something that will happen in the future they will move their eyes (while visualising) to the right.

There are other ways people cognitively process time (for example, some people visualise a line that stretches from 'behind' them and moves through them in a forward direction), but, if you are presenting to a large group, it's safe to assume that the majority of your audience will share a timeline that moves from left to right. Once you understand how our brain processes time you can use this as a powerful tool when speaking or presenting in order to influence and reinforce your message. By sorting 'past' events on the left and 'future' to the right, you will match their unconscious timeline and reinforce your message. But remember that in order for you to 'match' the audience's timeline you will be reversing your own which may well feel unnatural to you.

You can use timelines in your presentations:

➡ When you want to make clear distinctions between important information.

➡ To help your audience mentally separate and sort information.

➡ To create positive emotional 'anchors' for the toward emotions – achievement, anticipation, success.

➡ To separate and 'contain' difficult emotions the group may have experienced – loss, anxiety, disappointment, change, etc.

➡ When communicating change in business.

Left	Right
Past	Future
Bad news	Good news
Poor results	Anticipated results
Problems, difficulties	Plans, actions, solutions
Logic	Storytelling, metaphor
One department, site, business	Another department site, business
Old products, services	New products, services
Intellectual knowledge	Skills, behaviours
	Call to action

Use the stage

Use the stage as a tool in your presentation to help your audience sort information and emotion. Create specific areas on the stage where you talk about challenges, issues or problems and then consciously move to another area when you talk about future, solutions, actions, etc. This will help people cognitively sort your messages and create different emotional anchors where your audience will (unconsciously) feel toward and away from emotions and motivations.

There are a number of different visual aids which you can use to enhance the effect. These could include two different flip-charts in different areas or the stage (see Fig. 6.2), screens with different PowerPoint presentations, exhibits on different wall spaces or just different colour pens.

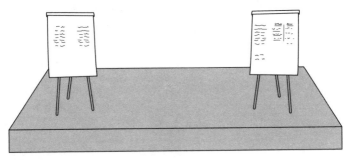

FIGURE 6.2 Use physical space to reinforce your message.

Here are some Dos and Don'ts for successful presentations.

Ways to lose influence in presentations	Ways to gain influence in presentations
Launch into your presentation without a clear, structured approach.	Prepare your first 60–90 seconds. Script it. Practise it in the mirror. Record it on your phone and play it back to yourself.
Risk: you lose the attention of the audience quickly and you come across as disorganised.	**Result**: you feel confident and get off to a strong start.

Lack of eye contact with the audience. Looking over people's heads to the back of the room.	Make eye contact with members of the audience. This will calm your nerves and create connection and empathy. Hold eye contact for three seconds (shorter and you fail to connect, longer and it starts to be uncomfortable).
Risk: you fail to gain emotional connection with your audience.	**Result**: this will calm your nerves and create empathy and connection.
You move around the stage in an attempt to avoid eye contact and to calm yourself down.	Find a comfortable location on the stage, adopt a strong balanced posture and stand still for much of your presentation.
Risk: you appear nervous and this is distracting to your audience.	**Result**: you have more gravitas and authority.
You lean more on one leg, put your hands in your pocket, or behind your back, lean on a table or stand behind a podium.	Stand evenly on both legs. Hold something in your hand to give you a focus and prevent you from putting hands in pockets.
Risk: you appear overly casual but nervous.	**Result**: you feel stronger and more confident.
You read out the words on your slides.	Your slides should have no more than three short bullet points (maximum). Let your audience read your slides at their own pace.
Risk: you lose impact. Reading over the top of your audience is distracting.	**Result**: your audience is able to concentrate and absorb information.
You look at the PowerPoint slides along with your audience.	Give your audience time to read and digest information. Take short pauses to look at your audience, breathe and connect. Wait until their eyes come back to you.
Risk: you miss the opportunity of connecting with your audience.	**Result**: you have time to relax, breathe and prepare.

▶

You have lots of dense text on your slides that you expect your audience to read while you talk over the top of them.	People cannot listen and read at the same time. Put complex information in a handout.
Risk: you confuse and bore your audience.	**Result**: your audience feel relaxed and engaged.
You speak quickly and don't include enough pauses.	Breathing and pausing gives you and your audience time to think and digest your message.
Risk: your audience feel rushed and anxious and they cannot assimilate your message.	**Result**: you and your audience feel relaxed and calm and you can connect and influence.

7th rule of influence in every channel:

In presentations, use the stage, room or space to reinforce your message.

Tips for presentations:

1. If you have an important presentation it's worth investing in a voice and body coach to help you prepare and get professional feedback, advice and support.

2. Practise your speech or presentation in front of your friends or colleagues and ask for honest feedback.

3. Watch great speakers on Ted.com and notice what they do to connect with their audience.

4. For a comprehensive set of affordable download tools on presentation skills go to: The Gravitas Method (http://thegravitasmethod.com/).

Influencing on the phone

The telephone is a great channel for influencing people as it gives you the opportunity to build understanding, rapport and to pick up on vocal and other cues from the other person. It's also an opportunity to develop your voice as a tool of influence. Many organisations rely on conference calls to connect virtual teams together; a lot of coaching takes place over the phone and we all need to sell, persuade and influence on one-to-one phone calls. Here are some ways to lose and gain influence during conference calls and one-to-one phone calls.

Conference calls	
Ways to lose influence on conference calls	**Ways to gain influence on conference calls**
Not being clear about what you want to achieve from the call.	Decide what you want from the call and be clear about your purpose.
Being late or unprepared. This often interrupts the whole group with an automated caller announcement.	Always be on time. Be one of the first on the line so you have time to relax and greet people as they join the call.
Thinking you can 'half listen' – type, pick up messages or emails, put the phone on mute while you do something else.	Give the same quality of attention you would if you were in the room. Find a comfortable seat and commit yourself to the call.
Forgetting who's on the call.	Draw a picture of a table on a page and write down each person's name so you can imagine them in the room. This will help when you need to get feedback or input on an idea or decision.

▶

Presenting one-way, long, informational updates and expecting others to stay focused (this rule applies for all meetings).	Send pre-reads and turn the agenda into questions for people to think about before the call.
Thinking a conference call is the same as a meeting. Conference calls can never replace face-to-face meetings; invest in getting together at least once a year to build team understanding, cohesion and team spirit.	Treat the medium with care. Make conference calls as short as possible and recognise that it takes even more concentration from your audience.

One-to-one calls	
Ways to lose influence on one-to-one calls	**Ways to gain influence on one-to-one calls**
Being late or unprepared.	Always be on time. Decide what you want the other person to think, feel and do after the call.
Think the other person can't pick up your emotional cues.	Prepare your emotional state: positive, energised, focused and committed.
Over-run on the call if you have agreed a time.	Always finish on time. If the other person wants to continue allow them to invite you. Assume they have another meeting to go to and respect the time you have been given.
Talk too quickly. Be monotone.	Develop musicality in your vocal range, especially on the phone, as it's your most potent tool of influence. Vary your tone and pitch. Speak clearly.
Waffle and be unclear about what you want. The phone makes it easy to have notes in front of you, or a mind map of what you want to cover.	Be succinct and to the point. Take only as much time as you absolutely need.

Brain Rules:

1. Information overload reduces memory retention, creativity and decision-making:

    ➡ Simplify, shorten, summarise.

2. Mirror neurons spread emotion:

    ➡ Tune up your emotional state to influence others.

    ➡ Tune in to others and positively shift their emotions.

3. Fight–flight mode causes the brain to shut down:

    ➡ First get your audience to relax and move into parasympathetic mode.

    ➡ Tell stories and use metaphor to convince, persuade and inspire.

Top Tips:

1. Set your intention and then design everything you do to help you achieve that.

2. Be fully present (especially in meetings or on the phone when it can be tempting to 'switch off').

3. Remember emotions sell – everything; use stories, metaphors and images and speak from the heart.

4. Practise the tools from this text. Try new things out. See what works best for you.

5. Practise a little mindfulness every day: it will train your brain to stay calm and focused.

6. Enjoy the journey.

Chapter 7

Influence under pressure

I've learned that people will forget what you said, people will forget what you did, but people will never forget how you made them feel.

Maya Angelou

Outline

This chapter will give you the tools to be influential under pressure and in challenging situations.

1. How to influence difficult people

2. Emotional flooding

3. How to influence when there's not enough time

How to influence difficult people

We all have to deal with people we find difficult. Sometimes it's a boss who you feel is preventing you from progressing or who's critical, sometimes it's a customer who never seems to be satisfied, or a colleague who feels like a thorn in your side, but managing these challenging relationships is both a test of influence and a great opportunity to increase it. The truth is that it's easy to influence people who are like us, or who we get on with, but our ability to be truly influential comes into play when we dig deep and find new skills to deal with these challenges.

If you've ever called up a company frustrated, irritated, short-tempered or angry and been met with somebody on the other end of the phone who is able to calm you down and make you feel better you will have experienced the verbal jujitsu of an empathetic and skilled listener; or if somebody gave you a new perspective and helped you find a solution when you thought you'd exhausted all the possibilities; or asked you a simple question that suddenly changed everything for you. These are the martial artists of influence, people who have practised, adapted and learnt along the way.

> **1st rule of influence under pressure:**
>
> Build your flexibility. Try out new behaviours, new approaches and new thinking.

The first place to begin is with you

The word *difficult* is the place to start. Unpack the word and get really clear about what specifically you find difficult. Is it things they say? Is it their tone of voice? Is it what they are doing? Once we label someone as difficult we can begin to 'fix' them in our mind and it can become a self-fulfilling prophecy. So start by working out the specific behaviours you find challenging; this helps to separate out the positive behaviours from the ones you find difficult. When is the person not difficult? Do other people find them easier to get on with than you do? What's their secret? But first, it's important to look at whether there's something about our own behaviour we can change because that's a much easier place to start.

Hot buttons

Sometimes people's behaviour triggers our own unconscious emotional responses. We may have grown up with a sibling who treated us in a particular way that we found patronising and irritating and this person unconsciously triggers our associations with that sibling. Or a parent may have been overly critical or dismissive and we feel that our boss is exactly the same. Think about what emotional or memory triggers the behaviour touches on. Do they remind you of someone else? If they do, you can be sure that they are hitting your own hot buttons. So what can you do if that's the case?

Calibrated loops

Calibrated loops are ways of reacting that are deeply coded into our brain's neural pathways because we've been practising them since we were children. For instance, your boss may use a certain tone of voice that one of your parents used when you were 'in trouble' (and remember, that for many people the boss is an unconscious trigger for a parent figure). In a split second, your brain travels down the familiar neural pathways it's travelled your whole life and before you know it you feel defensive and start to challenge or argue. And if you react defensively, unless your boss has great emotional regulation, he (or she) is likely to become more directive in response (even more like a parent) and this may spark even stronger feelings of needing to argue and defend.

The problem with this is that our emotions (through our mirror neuron system) are two-way feedback systems where one person's reaction sparks the other's in an escalating spiral. We sometimes replay a 'life script' which is an unconscious but familiar response to what somebody else says or does because it reminds us of something we experienced as children. Have you ever wondered why an innocent comment can sometimes end up in a full-blown argument but you couldn't work out why? It's most likely that it was not so much *what* was said but the emotional hot buttons that kicked off an unconscious response. So if this happens with the person you find difficult you need to find a way to step out of the loop.

There are many ways we can do this, but the solution that works for you in one situation might not work as well in another. Sometimes it will depend on the strength of your emotional trigger, or on the strength of the other person's response. No two people or two situations are exactly the same so think about what might work best for you in your particular situation. If you try something and it doesn't work try another approach. Remember that influence is a set of skills, behaviours and attitudes that we hone and practise. Here are some emotional circuit breakers that you can use.

2nd rule of influence under pressure:

Step out of the calibrated loop.

Circuit breaker 1: Manage your emotional state

If you notice that the calibrated loop is operating in an important relationship, then set your intention before you next meet the person. Remember about the powerful effect of the mirror neuron system to transmit your emotions silently to the other person and think about what emotional state would be most useful in the context. Choosing to hold a feeling of respect for the other person (even if you don't like certain behaviours) is a good place to start. Respect creates an open emotional state between you. You might also start by saying something appreciative or positive to the person which will put them at ease right from the start. Using appreciation is a bit like the linguistic equivalent of approaching somebody with open palms to show you are unarmed, which will help them open up to what you have to say.

3rd rule of influence under pressure:

The person with the strongest emotional state influences the other person. Choose your emotions wisely.

Circuit breaker 2: Positive intention

At a deep level all our behaviour comes out of a positive intention. As children we learn how to survive by building habits of thinking and behaving. For some people, responding with aggression has become a learned form of defence; reacting with anger can be a way to shield them from attack (fear), or being critical and controlling is a way to regain a sense of security. Think about what might be driving the other person's behaviour. Are they afraid of losing control? Being seen as stupid? Do they fear losing face? Are they in fear of losing their job or positional power? All our behaviour at some level is driven by a need to survive, and when we hold this in mind we begin to have feelings of compassion rather than judgement about the other person's behaviour. Imagine the world through their eyes and become intensely curious about the situation; this helps you emotionally stand back. Ask yourself: 'What would have to be true for me to make me behave in that way?' You may be surprised with what you discover. You may find a new perspective on the situation. Curiosity will help you become more flexible in the choices you make.

4th rule of influence under pressure:

See beyond the behaviour to the emotion beneath. Negative emotions such as fear and anxiety may be the hidden issue.

If you find yourself being pulled into strong negative emotions, imagine you are watching yourself and the other person from above as if you are seeing the situation from a camera in the ceiling. This is a useful way of decoupling from the strong emotion and will stop you being drawn into a negative spiral. Becoming an observer will help you notice the dance that is happening between you; suddenly you notice that your body has become very tense, or you've broken eye contact and you're looking out the window. As soon as you notice the body language, tone of voice and the emotions you then have a choice to shift them. The calibrated loop can only continue to spin as long as we are unconscious of its power and are caught in its trap. Shift your body. Move. Stand up. Ask for a break. Get a glass of water. Do whatever you need to take a moment to shift the focus and help you get back on track.

5th rule of influence under pressure:

Stand back and become an observer to avoid being drawn into a negative emotional spiral.

Circuit breaker 4: Say it like it is

Another strategy is to name what's happening. For example, if you start to become argumentative you could say: 'We seem to be arguing about something that's important to both of us. How might we get back on track?' Or, 'I notice that we both have such different ways of approaching this issue, why don't we look at how we can find common ground?' 'Meta-commenting' involves moving your attention away from the *what* of your conversation to the *how* of your conversation.

Meta-commenting is something that coaches often use, and it is a powerful skill to put in your toolkit of influence. It can take courage because it's more common to avoid admitting that there may be underlying and unresolved conflict. Unless we have the courage to face what's really happening, we will be destined to repeat the same behaviour and get the same result. If you notice that conversations get stuck in familiar negative patterns, consider whether you can interrupt the pattern of behaviour and build a more productive and positive relationship. Use liberating presuppositions when you do make a meta-comment; the examples above contain the presuppositions that it is possible to 'get back on track', that you 'share common ground' and that you can resolve this together.

6th rule for influence under pressure:

Use positive presuppositions to shift the attention to a positive outcome.

Circuit breaker 5: Stand up *for* yourself but not *against* them

There are times when influence is about standing up for you but not *against* the other person. Have you ever learnt a tough lesson? Has anyone ever told you a truth that set you on a new path? That's a gift of true influence. But standing up in a non-defensive, positive way can be a challenge if the other person has positional power over us and we rely on them for survival (a boss, a teacher or someone in authority). If this is the case, our reactions can move from fight – becoming aggressive or stonewalling; flight – avoiding the person, or even leaving a job; or freeze – being unable to respond or act.

Case study

My own habit under significant emotional threat was to go into freeze; I literally stopped being able to hear what was said, to think clearly or even see clearly. So I had to learn a new way of responding. My chance to practise came when I was working with someone whose habit was to bully, criticise and play 'top dog'. At the time, I was seeing a wonderful coach who encouraged me to arrange a conversation with this person and say calmly but assertively that her behaviour was not acceptable and that I would no longer tolerate it. That was really tough for me. I'd perfected my freeze response over many years and the very idea of going back into (what felt like) the lion's den for another mauling struck dread into my heart. I needed to practise and prepare my emotional state. I visualised the conversation going the way I hoped it would and practised being concise and avoiding getting pulled into justifying, arguing or criticising. When the day came it was still a big challenge, but it was one of the best lessons I ever had. I learnt a new behavioural skill and realised that if I had the courage to do it once I could do it again when I needed to. I also learnt that confidence and influence are step-by-step processes and that the hardest challenges are often the best way to learn.

If you do have a big, scary challenge, ask someone you trust to help you practise. Coach them on how you think the other person might respond and play out different scenarios so you can be more prepared for whatever happens. Ask your friend to give you honest feedback about how you come across; your body language, voice tone, eye contact as well as your words. Discover the non-verbal messages you communicate and think about how to use these to positively affect the interaction. The more you practise and hone what you want to say, the more confident you will be when you're with the other person. Set your intention to be respectful but firm. Get the support of your friend before and after the meeting and you can imagine them being in the room with you for moral support.

7th rule of influence under pressure:

Stand up *for* you but not *against* the other person.

Circuit breaker 6: Values

Explore what common values you share with the other person. Finding common ground around values can help to reconnect you with that person and builds a sense of understanding and rapport. Before you next meet with the person take some time and ask yourself:

➡ What's really important to them?

➡ What do you both want?

➡ Do you share a common goal (to complete a project, make your business successful or bring an idea to life)?

➡ Can you focus on the values that you share to frame your conversation with them?

➡ What else might be happening for that person that may be affecting their behaviour? Are they under stress which may be pushing them into negative responding?

> **8th rule of influence under pressure:**
>
> Keep an open mind and an open heart.

Circuit breaker 7: Create neutral ground

Facing somebody while holding eye contact can feel threatening and trigger a fight–flight response if you are nervous or it's a high-stakes meeting. It's easy to create neutral ground by sitting side by side, and the way you can do this is to bring in a report or document to review together. This will allow you to adjust your position to sit side by side. If you need to discuss a contractual disagreement, you can use the copy of the physical contract to point to when talking about the contentious issue – this helps to place the disagreement *onto* the contract not *into* the other person. When emotions are running high you can sit or stand side by side which will help to reduce eye contact and de-escalate any feelings of threat but, because you are physically close, you can still maintain rapport.

Walking side-by-side is another way to create neutral ground and build rapport. Go for a walk somewhere in nature (a local park will do) or head out to a coffee shop if you're at work. Walking moves you into a more parasympathetic brain state (walking releases oxygen into your blood and helps your brain think more clearly; reduces the hormones cortisol and adrenaline in your system; and reduces stress and uses up some of your nervous energy). Deliberately match the other person's walking pace and energy and move into step with them to create a stronger sense of connection between you.

> **9th rule of influence under pressure:**
>
> Create neutral space to calm emotions while maintaining connection with the other person.

Emotional flooding

There are times when we experience what's known as emotional flooding when we're momentarily incapable of using any of the above strategies because we're locked into a primitive and overwhelming emotional response. So what's the cause of these more debilitating responses and what can we do about them?

Emotional flooding is a physical stress response we have when we feel we are being attacked. This is our evolutionary survival response to threat and, while it was useful when we faced predators, in our modern world our heightened stress response can prevent us thinking clearly and responding appropriately and can lock us into intense anxiety, fear or anger. A modern-day example of emotional flooding is the feelings of rage people experience on the roads when they explode into irrational and extreme acts of aggression. When people are in the grip of such an emotional hijacking, their brain releases adrenaline into the bloodstream which increases the heart rate to around 90–100 beats per minute; breathing increases, digestion slows down and their brain and body is overloaded with stress hormones (people often feel 'out of their body'). And until the stressful situation is resolved, the heart rate remains elevated, the body continues to pump out adrenaline and people remain on 'red alert'. The body takes around 20 minutes before the neurotransmitters can reset the system and the heart rate returns to normal. Because many of us experience daily stresses our stress tolerance is reduced over time and we can experience a more intense stress response more quickly. So what can we do?

How to deal with emotional flooding

The best response to emotional flooding is to take all the pressure off. Think of it like a flood: it needs to run its course before the waters subside. We often need a day or two to recover from a strong emotional experience but we can speed up the rate of emotional recovery by doing things that help the brain regain equilibrium and by resetting the body's physiology.

If you are a leader or manager of a team and one of your team members responds in such a powerfully emotional way make sure you help them regain their emotional equilibrium by taking all the pressure off. These situations, while painful for people at the time, are prime opportunities for being a true leader who demonstrates emotional awareness and insight. Dealing constructively with strong emotions at work is a way to build trust, safety, loyalty and commitment in the team. How do we take the pressure off and build habits that will increase our emotional resilience?

Exercise

Strong cardiovascular exercise will use up the adrenaline and reset your system more quickly. It can be a great release for feelings of anger or rage and helps to calm down the body. It will also help you sleep more easily if you are feeling particularly stressed.

Quiet time

Sometimes talking to others can keep you locked into the emotional flood because you re-live the experience every time you talk about it. When we're upset, we tend to be defensive and want to 'blame' the other person. So spend some time alone or alternatively talk to a trusted friend who has a cool head to get some support but who will help you move back into a more resourceful emotional state.

Perspective

When you are on the other side of the flood, take some quiet time to reflect and think about the things you did well, the things you would like to do differently next time and remind yourself that you've just had another lesson in becoming a black belt at influence. Ask yourself the following questions:

➡ What was the specific trigger?

➡ What meaning did you give to their actions, words or gestures? What conclusions did you come to?

➡ When you look back at other times you have responded with this particular emotion are there any common themes that emerge?

➡ Is it possible that your emotional trigger is partly caused by replaying a life script?

10th rule of influence under pressure:

Allow your brain to reset. Then take time to reflect and plan.

Getting back on track

Sometimes important relationships simply get a bit off track and, if these are people who are important to our success and to achieving our goals, we can make time to get them back into a more productive place. You might use an incisive question to kick off your conversation such as:

➡ Things seem to have gone a bit off the tracks between us (this is an example of a meta-comment). How can we get back on track?

➡ What do you need from me to help us build a better working relationship?

- ➡ How can we best achieve our common goals?

- ➡ How can we build a more successful working relationship?

- ➡ What are the ground rules we need to agree to make this work?

- ➡ What's the risk to the business (family, group, team) if we don't get the relationship back on track?

- ➡ What have I not noticed that you wished I had?

- ➡ What is it that we keep avoiding, that when we face together will help us achieve our outcome?

Initiating a conversation to resolve issues or conflict is a skill of positive influence. Once you become more skilled at these conversations you will become known as a positive, empathetic and courageous person.

11th rule of influence under pressure:

Be the one to start the difficult conversation and watch your star rise.

How to influence when there's not enough time

It's happened to all of us, we've spent weeks preparing for a meeting, conversation, presentation or sales opportunity and the person is late, has to leave early, or reduces the time you thought you had. It's easy to go into panic or to feel frustrated, angry or disappointed. All these feelings can get in the way and undermine your ability to get your message across. The more important the meeting is the more important it is to have a Plan B because we know that Plan A often gets pushed off course, particularly with important clients or senior managers. What can you do to stand the best chance of achieving your outcome?

The greater your sense of ease, the deeper your attention, the better you are able to listen to the other person and the more likely you are to leave a powerful positive impression of who you are. You will also increase the chance of a follow-up meeting, telephone call or conversation if your meeting has been called short. Remember that our ability to positively influence someone does not depend as much on the *amount* of time we have, but on the *quality* of the time we have with them.

12th rule of influence under pressure:

Slow down in order to speed up. Time to pause pays dividends.

Tips for handling pressure:

1. Connect with your body to move it back into a parasympathetic state as quickly as you can. Deep breathing releases oxytocin into your bloodstream and is one of the quickest and easiest ways to reduce stress. As soon as you begin to breathe more deeply your mind becomes clear and you can make every second count.

2. Become aware of your two big toes on the floor, focus your attention on how they connect with the ground, feel the movement of your ribs as you breathe to create a sense of physical ease in your body.

3. Accept the situation exactly as it is. You cannot change it, but you can change your attitude toward it. Tell yourself this was exactly what was meant to happen. It's a complete mystery but for some unknown reason this is the best outcome. Thinking in this way will move back to a positive feedback loop between thoughts and feelings and give you a sense of optimism.

4. If you only have a few minutes go straight for a relationship connection (forget all the facts and figures). Shake their hand,

look directly into their eyes and maintain eye contact for three seconds. As you hold eye contact, really 'see' the person. To help them to regain a sense of ease, particularly if they are under pressure, show your understanding of their situation and be empathetic.

5. The more important the meeting the more important it is to prepare for exactly this situation. Have your information on a single page. Or have a diagram to summarise your proposition. What's the 'frame' for your offering? What's your elevator pitch?

6. Ask questions: 'Given that time is a bit shorter, what is the single most important thing you need to get from me?' Or, 'What would make your life easier right now?' Or, 'What would be most helpful?'

Exercise

Here's an NLP (Neurolinguistic Programming) exercise to build your emotional resilience toolkit so you can better influence. You can use it when you face a significant challenge with either a difficult person or a difficult situation. You can think of it as a force-field or protective shell around you next time you are in the situation.

Alternatively, you could spend 10 minutes on it every day to build new habits of emotional resilience and confidence and help you remain present, responsive and able to act appropriately.

1. Go to a quiet, private space and draw an imaginary circle on the floor.

2. Stand on the outside of the circle and recall a powerful emotional state you would like to have in the situation (confidence, calm, clarity, fun, excitement, etc.). Select the emotional state that will help you achieve what you want and is the most appropriate for you.

3. Step into the circle and close your eyes.

4. Recall a time when you felt that emotion most powerfully. Feel all of the sensory connections you had in your body with that emotion. See if there are colours, sounds or sensations connected to that emotion. If there are, intensify these. Imagine you are the director of a movie and you can turn up any of the elements in your mind – the colour, the sound and the feelings.

5. When you are deeply associated (feeling as if you are *in the emotion*) press your thumb and forefinger together for a few seconds to 'anchor' the feeling.

6. Step out of the circle and choose another powerful emotion you want to take with you into the situation. Then step into the circle and repeat the process as above.

7. Step out of the circle and choose a third powerful emotional state that will help you (you can take as many as you want, but find at least three to build up positive feelings). Step into the circle and anchor the next feeling.

8. Do this exercise for a few days (or few weeks) to prepare to perform at your best when under pressure.

Brain Rules:

1. Under stress automatic mental habits are triggered.

2. Other people can trigger our own unconscious 'life scripts' that send us down the emotional low road.

3. All behaviour has a positive intention: to avoid fear, pain or insecurity – these are human survival mechanisms.

4. We can train ourselves to respond rather than react which changes the brain (neuroplasticity).

Top Tips:

1. If you change the emotion you can change the outcome.

2. Investigate your own responses first.

3. You can step out of automatic behaviour by using a circuit breaker.

4. Keep experimenting, be kind to yourself and keep practising.

Further reading

Bar-On, R, Tranel, D, Denburg, N L and Bechara, A (2003) Exploring the neurological substrate of emotional and social intelligence, *Brain*, 126, 1790–1800.

Bargh, J A, Chen, M and Burrows, L (1996) The automaticity of social behavior: direct effects of trait concept and stereotype activation on action, *Journal of Personality and Social Psychology*, 71, 230–244.

Bargh, J A, Gollwitzer, P M, Lee-Chai, A, Barndollar, K and Trötschel, R (2001) The automated will: nonconscious activation and pursuit of behavioral goals, *Journal of Personality and Social Psychology*, 81, 1014–1027.

Barsade, S G (2002) The ripple effect: emotional contagion and its influence on group behaviour, *Administrative Science Quarterly*, 47, 644.

Beer, M and Norhia, N (2000) Cracking the code of change, *Harvard Business Review*, May–June.

Booker, C (2004) *The Seven Basic Plots*, Continuum.

Cameron, J (1994) *The Artist's Way*, Pan MacMillan.

Damasio, A (1994) *Descartes, Error*, Harper Collins.

Gilkey, R, Caceda, R and Kilts, C (2012) When emotional reasoning trumps IQ, *Harvard Business Review*, September.

Gordon, E (2000) *Integrative Neuroscience: Bringing Together Biological, Psychological and Clinical Models of the Human Brain*, CRC Press.

Hitchings, H (2013) The dark side of verbs-as-nouns, *The New York Times*, 5 April.

Iacoboni, M (2009) *Mirroring People: the science of empathy and how we connect with others*, Picador.

Kang, M J, Hsu, M, Krajbich, I M, Loewenstein, G F, McClure, S M, Wang, J T and Camerer, C F (2009) The wick in the candle of learning: epistemic curiosity activates reward circuitry and enhances memory, *Psychological Science*, 20(8), 963–973.

Kline, N (2009) *More Time to Think*, Fisher King.

Loewenstein, G (1994) The psychology of curiosity: A review and reinterpretation, *Psychological Bulletin*, 116, 75–98.

McClure, S M, Li, J, Tomlin, D, Cypert, K S, Montague, L M and Read Montague, P (2004) Neural correlates of behavioral preference for culturally familiar drinks, *Neuron*, 44(2), 379–387.

McGovern, M K (2005) The effects of exercise on the brain, http://serendip.brynmawr.edu/bb/neuro/neuro05/web2/mmcgovern.html [accessed August 2013].

Moss, R (2010) *Dreamgates*, New World Library.

Pashler, H (1994) Dual-task interference in simple tasks: data and theory, *Psychological Bulletin*, 116(2), 220–244.

Raine, A (2013) *The Anatomy of Violence*, Pantheon.

Ramachandran, V S (2011) *The Tell-tale Brain: A Neuroscientist's Quest for What Makes Us Human*, Norton.

Senge, P M (2001) Leadership in living organisations, in *Leading Beyond the Walls*, Hesselbein, F, Goldsmith, M and Somerville, I (eds), Jossey Bass, 73–90.

Siegel, D (2011) *Mindsight*, Oneworld Publications.

Waks, L (2008) Listening from silence: inner composure and engagement, *Phaideusis*, 17, 65–74.

Weston, D (2007) *The Political Brain*, Public Affairs.

Wilson, C (2012) Eye-contact detector found in the brain, *NewScientist*, http://www.newscientist.com/article/dn22386-eyecontact-detector-found-in-the-brain.html#.UgdmM2Jwa1s [accessed August 2013].

Index

Robertson, D. 55
Rooney, Wayne 20

sadness 12
self-awareness 15
selling, big picture – tips for 31
semantic networks 93–5
Senge, P. 86
sensory-specific language 120
serial processing 32
should, use of word 113
Siegel, D. 44
sitting position, side by side 182
somatosensory cortex 15
Stone, L 148
stories 115–45
  complexity – simplifying 126–7
storytelling 7
  change management 127–35
  compared with information,
    brain processes 125–6
  emotions 121
  framework 142–4
  science of persuasion 124–5
stress
  brain's response to 128–30,
    132–3
  reduction 187
stress hormones 10, 128, 129
surprise 12, 121, 141
sweet spot 3, 4
sympathetic nervous system 10

taglines 141
team talk, listening skills 78

telephone
  conference calls 169–70
  one-to-one calls 170
  use of 150, 169–71
thinking styles, and brain structure
  6
thoughts, and emotions 51
time restraints 186–7
Time, The magazine, most
    influential people 1–2
tobacco companies, use of framing
    107
top-down attention 65
'toward' people 30
trans derivational search 89
try, use of word 112–13

USA, politics, use of framing 106

values
  common 181
  listening for 71
visualisation 19–20, 22, 23
  athletes – case study 19–20
  effect on brain 19–20, 22
voice tone 72

Waks, L 70
walking
  benefits of 24, 53
  side by side 182
Weston, D., *The Political Brain*
    138–40
Woods, Tiger 136